The St. Martin's Pocket Guide to Research and Documentation

The St. Martin's Pocket Guide to Research and Documentation
Third Edition

ADAPTED FROM

The St. Martin's Handbook
Fifth Edition

ANDREA A. LUNSFORD
MARCIA MUTH

BEDFORD / ST. MARTIN'S
Boston ♦ New York

Copyright © 1999, 2001, 2003 by Bedford/St. Martin's

All rights reserved. No part of this book may be reproduced, stored in a retrieval system, or transmitted in any form or by any means, electronic, mechanical, photocopying, recording, or otherwise, except as may be expressly permitted by the applicable copyright statutes or in writing by the Publisher.

First edition, 1995.

Manufactured in the United States of America.

8 7 6 5 4
f e d c b

For information, write: Bedford/St. Martin's, 75 Arlington Street, Boston, MA 02116 (617-399-4000)

ISBN: 0-312-39832-8

Acknowledgments

Page 22: Screenshot of Stanford University Library homepage. Courtesy of Stanford University, www.stanford.edu; **pages 24–26:** Screenshots of "simple search" for "film and hero" in the University of Kansas Libraries Web site. Courtesy of the University of Kansas Libraries, www.ku.edu; **page 31:** Screenshot of "ERIC" as accessed through the Cambridge Scientific Association Internet Database Service. Courtesy of CSA, www.csa3.com; **pages 37–38:** Screenshots of Yahoo! advanced search. Text and artwork copyright © 2003 Yahoo! Inc. All rights reserved. Yahoo! and the Yahoo! Logo are trademarks of Yahoo! Inc. Used with permission; **page 120:** Jewel Kilcher, "Amen": © 1995 WB Music Corp. (ASCAP) and Wiggly Tooth Music. All rights administered by WB Music Corp. All rights reserved. Used by permission. Warner Bros. Publications, U.S. Inc., Miami, Fl. 33014; **page 125:** Mary Pickford photo: Baron De Meyer/MPTV.net. Reproduced by permission; **page 133:** *Face/Off* photo of Nicholas Cage and John Travolta: Reproduced by permission of Photofest, Inc.

Contents

Introduction *1*

1 Preparing for a Research Project **3**

Narrowing and Focusing a Topic   *3*
Investigating What You Already Know about Your Topic   *4*
A Preliminary Research Plan   *5*
A Working Bibliography   *6*
■ *Keeping a Working Bibliography*   *7*

2 Conducting Research **10**

Kinds of Sources   *10*
Print and Internet Sources   *10*
Primary and Secondary Sources   *11*
Scholarly and Popular Sources   *12*
Older and More Current Sources   *13*
Kinds of Searches   *13*
Searches Using Online Library Resources   *14*
Catalog and Database Searches: Subject Headings and Keywords   *14*

Internet Searches: Subject Directories and Search Engines 15
Gathering Background Information 16
Guides to Reference Materials 16
Encyclopedias 17
Biographical Resources 17
Almanacs, Yearbooks, and Atlases 19
Using the Library 20
The Library Catalog 21
Indexes to Books and Reviews 26
Indexes to Newspapers, Magazines, and Journals 27
Bibliographies 30
Other Library Resources 32
Special Collections and Archives 32
Audio, Video, and Art Collections 32
Government Documents and Statistical Sources 32
Interlibrary Loans 33
Using the Web 33
Search Tools 33
■ SEARCH TOOLS 34
Keywords, Boolean Operators, and Quotation Marks 35
Online Libraries, Governmental and News Sites, and Periodicals 40
Reference Sources about the Internet and the World Wide Web 42

3 Evaluating Sources and Taking Notes 44

Evaluating Potential Sources for
   Usefulness and Credibility 44
■ SOME GUIDELINES FOR EXAMINING POTENTIAL SOURCES 46
Reading Sources with a Critical Eye 48
Reading with Your Research Question in Mind 48
Analyzing the Author's Stance and Tone 48
Assessing the Author's Argument and Evidence 49
Questioning Your Sources 49
Interpreting Sources: Synthesizing Data
   and Drawing Inferences 49

- *TAKING ACCURATE NOTES   50*
- *TAKING QUOTATION NOTES   51*
- *TAKING PARAPHRASE NOTES   51*
- *TAKING SUMMARY NOTES   52*
- *KNOWING WHEN TO QUOTE, PARAPHRASE, OR SUMMARIZE   53*

4   Acknowledging Sources and Avoiding Plagiarism   54

Which Sources to Acknowledge   54
Materials That Don't Require Acknowledgment   54
Materials That Require Acknowledgment   55
Academic Integrity and Plagiarism   57
Inaccurate or Incomplete Citation of Sources   57
Intentional Plagiarism   58
Tips for Using Sources   58

5   Research in the Humanities   60

Resources in the Humanities   60
Indexes and Databases for the Humanities   60
Web Resources for the Humanities   60
Art and Architecture   61
Classics   64
History   65
Literature   69
Music   71
Philosophy and Religion   72
Theater and Film   74
MLA Style   75
MLA Format for In-Text Citations   76
- *DIRECTORY TO MLA STYLE   76*
MLA Format for Explanatory and Bibliographic Notes   85
MLA Format for a List of Works Cited   86
Books   86

Periodicals 95
Electronic Sources 99
Other Kinds of Sources 109
A Student Research Essay, MLA Style 114
Chicago Style 144
■ DIRECTORY TO CHICAGO STYLE 144
Chicago Format for In-Text Citations, Notes, and Bibliography 145
Chicago Format for Notes and Bibliographic Entries 147
Books 148
Periodicals 151
Electronic Sources 152
Other Sources 155
A Student Research Essay, Chicago Style 157

6 Research in the Social Sciences 169

Resources in the Social Sciences 169
General Reference Sources for the Social Sciences 169
Indexes and Databases for the Social Sciences 169
Web Resources for the Social Sciences 170
Anthropology 171
Business and Economics 172
Communications, Journalism, and Linguistics 175
Education 177
Ethnic Studies 179
Geography 183
Law and Criminal Justice 184
Political Science 186
Psychology 189
Sociology and Social Work 191
Women's Studies 192

APA Style 194
■ *Directory to APA Style* 194
APA Format for In-Text Citations 196
APA Format for Content Notes 200
APA Format for a List of References 201
Indentation Style 202
Books 203
Periodicals 205
Electronic Sources 207
Other Sources 212
A Student Research Essay, APA Style 214

7 Research in the Natural and Physical Sciences and in Mathematics 226

Resources in the Natural and Physical Sciences and in Mathematics 226
General Reference Sources for the Natural and Physical Sciences and for Mathematics 226
Indexes and Databases for the Natural and Physical Sciences and for Mathematics 227
Web Resources for the Natural and Physical Sciences and for Mathematics 227
Astronomy 228
Chemistry 230
Earth Sciences 231
Life Sciences 233
Mathematics 236
Physics 238
CBE Style 240
CBE Formats for In-Text Citations 240
CBE Formats for a List of References 241
■ *Directory to CBE Style for a List of References* 242
Books 243

Periodicals 245
Electronic Sources 247
A Student Research Proposal, CBE Style 251

8 Research in the Applied Sciences   259

Resources in the Applied Sciences   259
General Reference Sources for the Applied Sciences 259
Indexes and Databases for the Applied Sciences 259
Web Resources for the Applied Sciences 260
Agriculture 261
Computer Science 262
Engineering 263
Environmental Studies 266
AIP Style   268
■ *Directory to AIP Style 269*
AIP Format for In-Text Notes   270
AIP Format for a List of Notes   270
Books 270
Periodicals 272
Electronic Sources 273
Other Sources 274

Introduction

The St. Martin's Pocket Guide to Research and Documentation is designed to be small enough to keep in your backpack but big enough to provide speedy and reliable help as you work on research assignments. Specifically, this guide provides

- general advice on the research process:
    narrowing and focusing a topic
    finding and evaluating sources in the library and on the Web
    taking notes
    acknowledging sources and avoiding plagiarism
- general resource materials useful in many fields
- specialized resources useful in particular disciplines
- documentation guidelines for five styles:
    MLA (Modern Language Association)
    APA (American Psychological Association)
    CMS (*Chicago Manual of Style*)
    CBE (Council of Science Editors)
    AIP (American Institute of Physics)

- sample student research assignments that show how to incorporate research materials and document sources

In the lists of resource materials, print materials that are also available online or on CD-ROM are noted accordingly in parentheses. "Online by subscription" means that the online version requires a paid subscription; therefore you will probably want to access it through a library computer. If a Web address (URL) is given, the online version does not require a subscription.

1
Preparing for a Research Project

Narrowing and Focusing a Topic

Any topic you choose to research must be manageable—must suit the scope, audience, length, and time limits of your assignment. Making a topic manageable often requires narrowing it, but narrowing is not always sufficient in itself. Rather than simply reduce a large subject to a smaller one, then, *focus* on a particular slant. The result of the narrowing and focusing process should be a research question that can be tentatively answered by a hypothesis, a statement of what you anticipate your research will show.

Like a working thesis, a hypothesis must be not only manageable but also interesting and specific. In addition, it must be arguable, a debatable proposition that can be proved or disproved by research evidence. For example, a statement like this one is not arguable since it merely states a widely known fact: "Senator Joseph McCarthy attracted great attention with his anti-Communist crusade during the 1950s." On the other hand, this statement is an arguable hypothesis since it can be proved or disproved: "Roy Cohn's political views and biased research while he was an assistant to Senator Joseph McCarthy were largely responsible for McCarthy's anti-Communist crusade."

In moving from a general topic of interest, such as Senator Joseph McCarthy's anti-Communist crusade of the 1950s, to a useful hypothesis, such as the one in the previous paragraph, you first narrow the topic to a single manageable issue, such as Roy Cohn's role in the crusade. After background reading, you then raise a question about that issue ("To what extent did Cohn's political views and research contribute to McCarthy's crusade?") and devise a possible answer, your hypothesis. The hypothesis that tentatively answers the research question must be precise enough to be supported or challenged by a manageable amount of research.

As you gather information and begin reading sources your research question is likely to be refined, and your hypothesis is likely to change significantly. Only after you have explored it, tested it, and sharpened it by reading and writing does the hypothesis become a working thesis.

In doing your research, you may find that your interest shifts, that a whole line of inquiry is unproductive, that a work you need to complete an argument is not available, or that your hypothesis is simply wrong. In each case, the process of research pushes you to learn more and more about your hypothesis, to make it more focused and more precise, to become an expert on your topic.

Investigating What You Already Know about Your Topic

Once you have narrowed and focused a topic, you need to marshal everything you already know about it. Here are some strategies for doing so:

- *Brainstorming.* Take five minutes to list, in words or phrases, everything you think of or wonder about your hypothesis. You may find it helpful to do this in a group with other students.
- *Freewriting in favor of your hypothesis.* For five minutes, write without stopping about every reason for believing your hypothesis is true.

- *Freewriting in opposition to your hypothesis.* For five minutes, write down every argument you can think of, no matter how weak or improbable, that someone opposed to your hypothesis might make.
- *Freewriting about your audience.* Write for five minutes about your readers, including your instructor. What do you think they currently believe about your topic? What sorts of evidence will convince them to accept your hypothesis? What sorts of sources will they respect?
- *Tapping your memory for sources.* List everything you can remember about *where* you learned about your topic: computer bulletin boards, email, books, magazines, courses, conversations, television. Much of what you know may seem like common knowledge, but common knowledge comes from somewhere, and "somewhere" can serve as a starting point for investigation.

A Preliminary Research Plan

Once you've considered everything you already know about your topic, you can begin to plan your research. To do so, answer the following questions:

- What kinds of sources (books, journal articles, videos, government documents, specialized encyclopedias, maps, illustrations, and so on) will you need to consult?
- Do you know the location and availability of the kinds of sources you need?
- How current do your sources need to be? (For topical issues, especially those related to science, current sources are usually most important. For historical subjects, older sources may still offer the best information.)
- Do you need to consult sources contemporary with an event or a person's life? If so, how will you get access to those sources?
- How many sources should you consult?

One major goal of your research plan is to begin building a strong working bibliography. Carrying out systematic research and keeping careful notes on the sources you find will make developing your list of works cited (see Chapters 5–8) much easier later on.

A Working Bibliography

Your working bibliography—a list of articles, books, Web sites, and other sources that you may ultimately use for your paper—is a key component of your research project. The emphasis here is on *working* because the list will probably include materials that end up not being useful. For this reason, you don't absolutely need to put all entries into the specific documentation style you will use (see Chapters 5–8). If you do style your entries appropriately, however, that part of your work will be done when you prepare the final draft. If you have access to a bibliography software program such as Research Assistant or Take Note!, it will format the entries for you automatically.

If you are not using a bibliography software program, first decide on a format: a computer file you can store on a disc, index cards, or a notebook. If you use cards or notebook pages, record information on only one side so that you can arrange your entries alphabetically when preparing your final list of works cited. Remember, too, that you should record source information for any material you photocopy or download from an electronic source. Be aware that not every source will provide the documentation information you may want. For example, a Web page might not list an author, so sometimes you'll need to work with the limited bibliographic information you do have. The checklists that follow will help you keep track of the information you should try to find and record for each kind of source. Note that some items in each category will not apply to all sources in that category. For example, not all periodicals have volume or issue numbers.

KEEPING A WORKING BIBLIOGRAPHY

1. For each *print book,* record all the following items that apply:
   - Call number
   - Author(s) and editor(s)
   - Title and subtitle
   - Place of publication
   - Publisher
   - Year of publication
   - Other information (translator, volume, edition)
2. For each *part of a print book,* such as a preface, a chapter, or an essay within a collection, record all the following items that apply:
   - Call number of book
   - Authors(s) of part
   - Title of part
   - Author(s) and editor(s) of book
   - Title and subtitle of book
   - Place of publication
   - Publisher
   - Year of publication
   - Inclusive page numbers of part
   - Other information (translator, volume of book)
3. For each *article in a print periodical,* record all the following items that apply:
   - Call number of periodical
   - Author(s) of article

(continued)

- Title of article
- Name of periodical
- Volume number
- Issue number
- Date of issue
- Inclusive page numbers of article

For articles you find in bibliographies or periodical indexes, also list the name of the index in case you need to check the information again, and add the call number or other location information when you find the source in your library catalog.

4. For each *Internet source,* access the source and print it out or download it if possible. You will eventually need to put the information for any sources you use into the correct documentation style, but the printout or download can save you the interim step of copying the information by hand, and it also serves as a record in case the source changes or disappears. The printout, download, or other form of entry should include all the following items that apply:

- Author(s) of document
- Title of document
- Title of site
- Editor(s) of site
- Sponsor of site
- Publication information for print version of source
- Range or total number of pages, paragraphs, screens, or other sections, if numbering appears on screen
- Names of database and online service
- Date source was published online or last updated

(continued)

> - Date you accessed the source
> - Electronic address (URL)
> 5. For *other kinds of sources* (such as photographs, films, recordings, or works of art), list the items required by the documentation style you are using (see Chapters 5–8), and note where you found the information.
> 6. When you examine print sources you have found in a catalog, bibliography, or index, check the accuracy of your information by consulting the title and copyright pages of a book and the table of contents and first page of a journal or magazine. For an electronic source, check the homepage of a Web site or the beginning of the document.

If you do use a bibliography software program, you'll need to become familiar with its forms for entering source information. These forms usually ask for the same sorts of source information as in the checklist that begins on page 7. It's a good idea to complete the appropriate bibliography software form as soon as you find a source. And remember that accuracy is just as important when you're using software as it is when formatting a bibliography on your own: although most programs put the elements in the correct order, you still need to double-check other items, such as capitalization of titles, names of authors, and accuracy of dates.

2
Conducting Research

Kinds of Sources

Sources come in many shapes and sizes; they include data from interviews, surveys, or observations; books and articles both in print and online; Web homepages and newsgroup postings; film, video, and music; and images of all kinds. Before you begin your research project in earnest, then, it's worth taking time to consider some important differences among sources.

Print and Internet Sources

Making a distinction between print and Internet sources can be tricky because many sources on the Net are electronic versions of texts that also exist in print. Most material on the Internet, however, has no print equivalent. And most print texts, likewise, are never published online. Why is this distinction so important? For one thing, the complex system of peer review and editorial evaluation of print texts that has developed over centuries is not yet in place on the Internet. If you go to a scholarly book or an article in a scholarly journal, you can be fairly sure that the text has been sent out to an expert reader in that particular field of study for peer review—and oftentimes to two or three such readers—before being accepted for publication. Even for books and articles not intended for a scholarly audience, you can easily check on the reputation of the publisher or magazine or newspaper in which an article appears. On the Internet, some journals and magazines that are published only electronically do have peer-review and editorial processes in place. But for most online materials, reviewing and editorial oversight depend solely on the author of the text. As a result, you need to know whether a source exists only in electronic form and, if so, how much you can trust it.

Another important distinction between print and Internet sources is that the latter are generally much less stable. Since online sources can easily be changed or deleted from the Internet entirely, you need to make a copy (either print or electronic) so that you have a record of the original; you may need to check the original later for bibliographic information or to verify the accuracy of a quotation in your notes.

Perhaps the most important distinction, though, is the one made originally: most print sources simply do not exist online and vice versa. Even if you limit your research to the most reputable online sources, you are probably missing out on the great majority of potential sources just because they are available only in print. Especially if your topic involves research into events that occurred more than a decade ago, you need to consult print sources as well as electronic ones to avoid getting a superficial and skewed perspective on what's been written about those events.

Primary and Secondary Sources

Another important difference in sources is the one between primary sources, or firsthand knowledge, and secondary sources, information available from the research of others.

Primary sources are basic sources of raw information, including experiments, surveys, or interviews you conduct; notes from field research; works of art or other objects you examine; literary works you read; and eyewitness accounts, photographs, news reports, and historical documents (such as letters, diaries, household records, speeches, and so on).

Primary sources are literally all around you. Your grandmother's diary, for example, might serve as a powerful primary source in an essay about customs of the era in which she was young; early maps from your library's map collection might serve as primary sources for an essay on changing national borders. Local historical societies and museums also offer good sources of primary materials, and your campus library will hold primary sources in both its regular and special collections and archives. In addition, you can find primary sources online at sites such as American Memory, <www.lcweb2.loc.gov/ammem/>, a project of the Library of Congress that includes more than seventy collections of digitized documents, photos, sound recordings, moving pictures, and other items from U.S. history.

Secondary sources are descriptions or interpretations of primary sources, such as researchers' reports, reviews of books and films, biographies, encyclopedia articles, and so on. Often what constitutes a primary or secondary source depends on the purpose of your research. A critic's evaluation of a painting, for instance, is a secondary source for an essay on that painting, but it serves as a primary source for a study of that particular critic's writing.

Most research projects draw on both primary and secondary sources. A research-based essay on the effect of media on Volkswagen advertising patterns, for example, might draw on primary sources such as very early Volkswagen advertisements as well as secondary sources such as articles or books on how media have affected advertising.

Scholarly and Popular Sources

While general nonacademic sources like popular magazines can be helpful in getting started on a research project, you will usually want to depend more heavily on the work of scholars who are authorities in a particular field related to your topic. The work of such experts usually appears in specialized scholarly journals. Here are some features that distinguish scholarly journals from popular magazines (many of these distinctions apply to online periodicals as well as to those in print):

SCHOLARLY	POPULAR
Cover lists contents of the issue	Cover features a color picture
Title often includes the word *Journal*	*Journal* usually does not appear in title
Source found at the library	Source found at grocery stores, newsstands, and so on
Few commercial advertisements	Lots of advertisements
Authors identified with academic credentials	Authors are journalists or reporters, not experts
Summary or abstract appears on first page of article; articles are fairly long	No summary or abstract; articles are fairly short
Articles have bibliographies	No bibliographies included

Older and More Current Sources

Think about whether your research project calls for the use of older, historical sources or up-to-the-minute information. Most projects can benefit from both kinds of resources. But if you are examining a recent scientific discovery, you will want to depend primarily on contemporary sources; on the other hand, if you are writing about the historical events related to Toni Morrison's novel *Beloved*, you may depend primarily on older sources that come from that time period.

Kinds of Searches

Even when you have a general idea of what kinds of sources exist and which kinds you need for your particular research project, you still have to figure out the best ways to look for them. The library and the Internet give you a variety of options for searching for sources, some of which are more efficient and productive than others. All of these options will be explained in more detail later in the chapter, but before you begin your research, it's important to understand some of the basic differences among them.

Searches Using Online Library Resources

Sometimes beginning researchers assume that all the information they could possibly need is readily available on the Internet. Even if you consider only electronic sources, however, there's a lot more out there than what's on the Net—and more than your own computer can turn up. Your library's computers hold important resources that are either not available on the Web (many are on CD-ROM) or not easily accessible to students except through the library's own system. The most important of these resources is the library's own catalog of its holdings (mostly books), but college libraries also pay to subscribe to a large number of databases—electronic collections of information, such as indexes to journal and magazine articles, texts of news stories and legal cases, lists of sources on particular topics, and compilations of statistics—that students can access for free. Many of these databases offer the additional advantage of having been screened or compiled by editors, reference librarians, or other scholars, a characteristic not true of most of the materials you find on the Web. Later sections of this chapter will provide detailed information on how to conduct effective Web searches. But as a general rule, you will be wise to work with the electronic sources available to you through your college library before turning to the Web.

Catalog and Database Searches: Subject Headings and Keywords

Searching for sources in your library's online catalog and databases will be much more efficient if you use carefully chosen words to limit the scope of your search. The catalog and databases usually index their contents by author, by title, and by subject headings—a standardized set of words and phrases used to classify the subject matter of books and articles. (For books, most U.S. libraries use the *Library of Congress Subject Headings,* or LCSH, for this purpose.) When you search the catalog by subject, then, you are searching only one part of the electronic record of the library's books, and you will need to use the exact wording of the LCSH classifications. Searches using keywords, on the other hand, make use of the computer's ability to look for *any* term in *any* field of the electronic record, including not just subject but author, title, and, for articles, perhaps an abstract or summary of the article's content. Keyword searching is less restrictive, but it requires you to put some thought into choosing your search terms in order to get the best results. In addition, you need to learn to use the techniques of combining keywords and using parentheses and quotation marks to limit (or in some cases expand) your search.

Internet Searches: Subject Directories and Search Engines

The Internet has no overall index such as the LCSH (yet). Like library catalogs and databases, however, it offers two basic ways for you to search for sources related to a particular topic: one using subject categories and one using keywords. Most Internet search tools, such as Yahoo!, Lycos, and Google, offer both of these options. A subject directory organized by categories allows you to choose a broad category such as "Entertainment" or "Science" and then to click on increasingly narrow categories such as "Movies" or "Astronomy" and then "Thrillers" or "The Solar System" until you reach a point where you are given a list of Web sites or the opportunity to do a keyword search. (In the latter case, the computer searches for keywords appearing in Web sites.) With the second kind of Internet search option, a search engine, you start right off with a keyword search. Because the Internet contains vastly more material than even the largest library catalog or database, searching it using a search engine requires even more thought and care in the choosing and combining of keywords.

Gathering Background Information

Consulting reference works such as encyclopedias, biographical dictionaries and indexes, atlases, and so on is a good way to get started on your research project, even though the project will eventually take you beyond such general reference sources. These works are especially good for

- getting an overview of a topic
- identifying subtopics of interest to you
- leading you to more specialized sources
- identifying useful keywords for electronic searches

Guides to Reference Materials

Your library's reference collection includes two broad types of reference materials: those that are general in scope and those that deal with specific disciplines (music, zoology, political science, and so on). The following guides to reference works can help you identify those that suit your purpose.

Gale Directory of Databases. 1993–. Published yearly, this two-volume resource (one volume for online databases, the other for CD-ROM) is the most comprehensive index and guide to databases available.

Guide to Reference Books. 11th ed. 1996. This large book supplies annotated lists of general reference works and specialized bibliographies and is divided into five sections: General Reference; Humanities; Social and Behavioral Sciences; History and Area Studies; and Science, Technology, and Medicine. Each section is further subdivided into areas and then into special approaches. Full bibliographic information, including Library of Congress call number, is provided for each entry.

Walford's Guide to Reference Material. 7th ed. 2 vols. 1999. *Walford's* two volumes deal with Science and Technology; Social and Historical Sciences, Philosophy, and Religion; and Generalities, Languages, the Arts, and Literature.

Encyclopedias

For general background on a subject, encyclopedias are a good place to begin, particularly because many include bibliographies that can point you to more specialized sources. Though some encyclopedias provide in-depth information, more often they serve as a place to start, not as a major source of information. Note that many general encyclopedias are available, often in elegant multimedia, on CD-ROM or by online subscription from your library's site.

GENERAL ENCYCLOPEDIAS

Collier's Encyclopedia (CD-ROM)
The Columbia Encyclopedia (online by subscription)
EncyberPedia (online at <http://www.encyberpedia.com>)
Encyclopedia Americana (online by subscription)
The New Encyclopedia Britannica (online by subscription)

SPECIALIZED ENCYCLOPEDIAS

Compared with general encyclopedias, specialized encyclopedias—on subjects from ancient history to world drama—usually provide more detailed articles by authorities in the field, as well as extensive bibliographies for locating sources. Again, you should rely on these books more for background material than as major sources of information. Many specialized encyclopedias are available on CD-ROM or online as well as in print. For more information on specialized encyclopedias in particular fields, see Chapters 5–8.

Biographical Resources

The lives and historical settings of famous people are the topics of biographical dictionaries and indexes. If the person you are researching is dead, consider whether you want to consult a current volume covering deceased people or a volume covering living people that was published during your subject's lifetime. Here are a few examples of biographical reference works; many others, particularly volumes specialized by geographic area or field, are available.

African American Biographies. 1992–. Profiles over five hundred notable men and women.

American Men and Women of Science. 1989–. Formerly *American Men of Science.* Provides biographical information on notable scientists alive today.

Biography Index. 1946–; quarterly. Lists biographical material found in current books and over twenty-six hundred periodicals. (online by subscription, CD-ROM for July 1984–present)

Contemporary Authors. 1967–; annual. Supplies short biographies of authors who have published works during the year. (CD-ROM)

Current Biography. 1940–; monthly, with annual cumulations. Provides informative articles on people in current events. Includes photographs and short bibliographies. (online by subscription, CD-ROM, 1984–)

Dictionary of American Biography. 1927–37 and supplements. Contains biographies of over fifteen thousand deceased Americans from all phases of public life since Colonial days. Entries include bibliographies of sources.

Dictionary of National Biography. 1885–1900 and supplements through 1985. Covers deceased notables from Great Britain and its colonies (excluding the post-Colonial United States).

International Who's Who. 1935–; annual. Contains biographies of persons of international status.

Notable American Women: 1607–1950. 3 vols. 1972. Supplement, *Notable American Women: The Modern Period.* 1980. Contains biographies (with bibliographies) of women who contributed to North American society. The supplement covers women who died between 1951 and 1975.

Webster's New Biographical Dictionary. 1983–. Provides biographical information on important deceased people of the last five thousand years.

Who's Who. 1849–; annual. Covers well-known living British people. *Who Was Who,* with volumes covering about a decade each, lists British notables who died between 1897 and the present.

Who's Who in America. 1899–; biannual. Covers famous living North Americans. Notable Americans no longer living are in *Who Was Who in America,* covering 1607 to the present. Similar specialized works include *Who's Who of American Women, Who's Who of Black Americans, Who's Who in Government,* and so on.

Almanacs, Yearbooks, and Atlases

Almanacs, yearbooks, atlases, and other sources provide information on current events and statistical and geographic data.

ALMANACS, YEARBOOKS, NEWS DIGESTS

Facts on File: News Digest. 1941–; weekly. Summarizes and indexes facts about current events. (online by subscription, 1975–; CD-ROM, 1980–)

Information Please Almanac. 1947–; annual. Includes many charts, facts, and lists as well as short summaries of the year's events and accomplishments in various fields.

Statesman's Year-Book. 1863–; annual. Contains facts and helpful current statistics about agriculture, government, population, development, religion, and other topics in countries of the world.

Statistical Abstracts of the United States. 1878–; annual. Published by the Bureau of the Census: presents government data on population, business, immigration, and other subjects. (online, 1995–, at <http://www.census.gov/stata6/www>; CD-ROM, 1987–)

World Almanac and Book of Facts. 1868–; annual. Presents data and statistics on business, education, sports, government, population, and other topics. Includes institutional names and addresses and reviews important annual public events. (online by subscription, 1998–; CD-ROM in Microsoft® Bookshelf™)

ATLASES

In addition to physical maps of all parts of the world, the following atlases contain maps showing population, food distribution, mineral concentrations, temperature and rainfall, and political borders, as well as many other facts and statistics.

Atlas of World Cultures: A Geographical Guide to Ethnographic Literature. 1989.
Hammond World Atlas. 2002.
National Geographic Atlas of the World. 1999.
The Times Atlas of the World. 1999.
The Rand McNally Commercial Atlas and Marketing Guide. 2002.

Using the Library

The library is one of a researcher's best friends, especially in an age of electronic communication. Your college library houses a great number of print materials: books, periodicals, and reference works of all kinds. And, as noted earlier, computer terminals there give you access to electronic catalogs and databases—and access to many other libraries (both real and virtual) via the Internet. It is essential, then, to acquaint yourself with the resources in your own college library.

The most efficient way to learn about your library is to make an appointment with a reference librarian, who can introduce you to your library's resources and offer concrete tips on how to access them. If a librarian is not available, ask whether the library has an online self-tutorial that can help you learn about the library's resources. If you have your own computer and Internet connection, you can do some of your library research from home. In addition, you can no doubt access the library's resources from computer labs on campus.

In fact, one way to start learning about your library's resources is to visit its Web site, which you can usually access directly from your school's main site. Most library homepages include sections describing collections (often by subject and type), hours of operation, and a floor plan, as well as include links to each area of the library and to its databases. Visitors to the main library page at Stanford University, for instance, shown on page 22, can learn a lot about Stanford's online catalog (named Socrates) as well as about the many databases that the university's libraries subscribe to. In short, checking out the Web site can give you a good virtual tour of the library that you can then build on with a visit in person.

The Library Catalog

The library catalog lists all of the library's books, as well as its periodical holdings and subscriptions. Some libraries still have their catalogs on cards, but most have transferred (or are in the process of transferring) their files to an electronic catalog you can access easily.

Library catalogs follow a standard pattern of organization. Each holding is identified by three kinds of entries: one headed by the *author's name,* one by the *title,* and one or (usually) more by the *subject.* If you can't find a source under one of these headings, try the others; sometimes entries are lost or misfiled. If your library's catalog is electronic, it can also be searched using *keywords*; in most catalogs, the computer can identify sources in which the keywords appear either in the title or in the subject headings under which the source is classified.

IDENTIFYING SUBJECTS FOR YOUR SEARCH

Subjects in the library catalog are usually identified and arranged according to the system presented in the *Library of Congress Subject Headings* (LCSH). This multivolume work may be kept at the reference desk and is also available online. In it, you can check the exact wording of subject headings and define key terms of interest to you. You may find that the LCSH identifies headings that have not readily occurred to you. Under most headings, you'll find other subjects that are treated (identified by *UF,* "use for"), broader headings that include the subject (*BT,* "broader topic"), and narrower headings that might be relevant (*NT,* "narrower topic").

22 Conducting Research

A Library Homepage

An Electronic College Catalog Search: Search Page

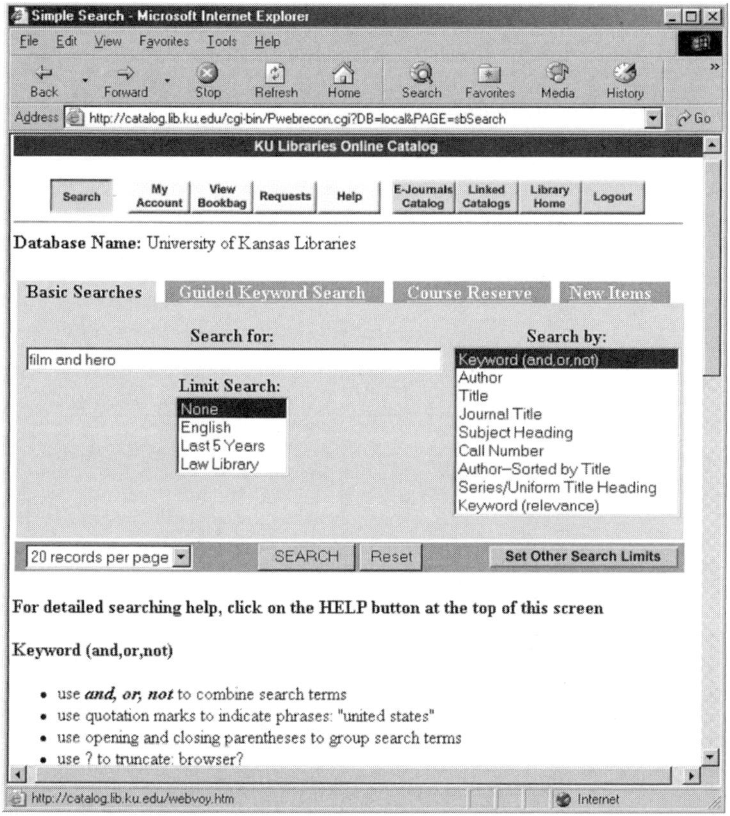

The illustrations on pages 23–25 show how the library electronic catalog at the University of Kansas was searched using the combined keywords "film" and "hero." The first screen shows the "simple search" page on which a student has entered these keywords. This search found

An Electronic College Catalog Search: Results List

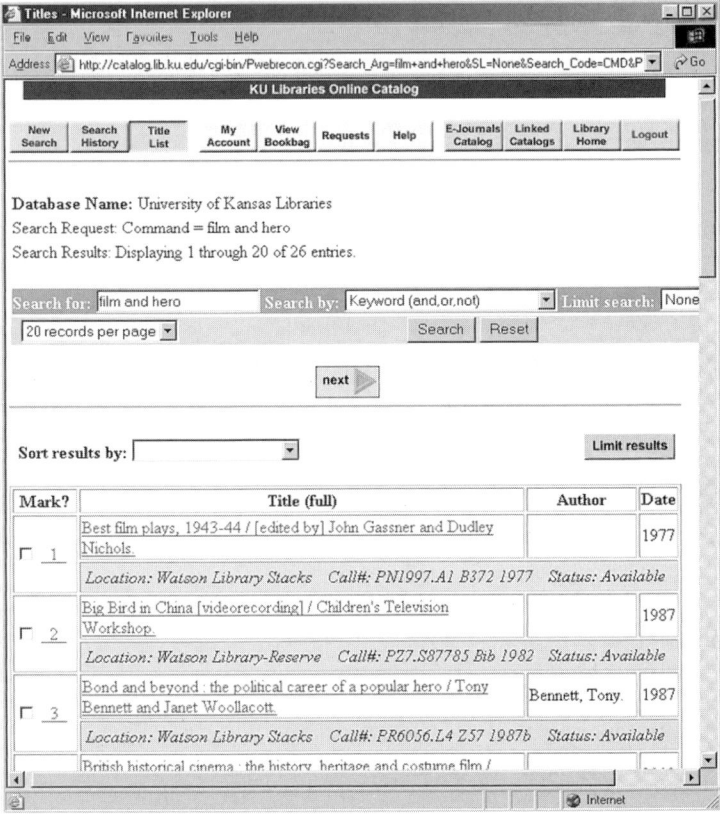

twenty-six catalog entries containing those words; the second screen shows the beginning of these search results, listed alphabetically by title. Clicking on a title takes you to the catalog page showing the "full

An Electronic College Catalog Search: "Full Record" for a Book

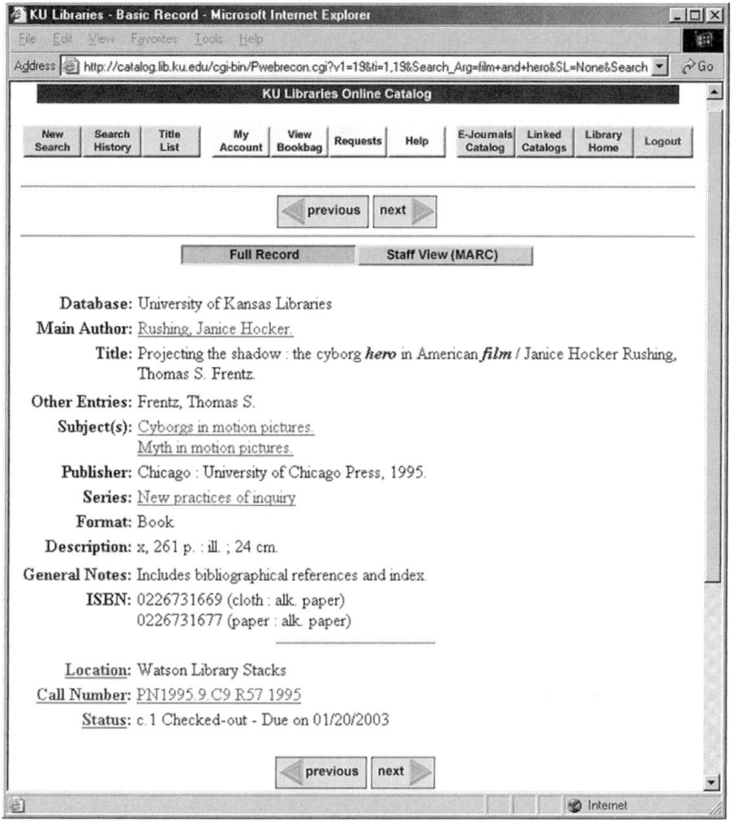

record" for that book; the third screen shows an example of one of these records, including the location of the book within the library system and the information that it was checked out, along with the due date. Note also that the subject headings under which this book is classified, "Cyborgs in motion pictures" and "Myth in motion pictures," are links that you could click on to take you to lists of other books in the catalog that are classified under those headings.

Searching only for subject entries is likely to be inefficient, however, because the headings are usually so broad. If the best Library of Congress heading you can identify does not match your particular needs or is so broad that your search yields many books but only a few that are useful, use other leads. Look to bibliographies, book indexes, periodical indexes, and notes in other publications for potentially useful authors and titles.

USING CALL NUMBERS TO LOCATE BOOKS

Besides identifying a book's general location within the library, each catalog entry also lists a call number—the book's identification number. Most academic libraries now use the Library of Congress system, which begins call numbers with letters of the alphabet.

Once you have printed out the catalog entry for the book or written down the call number, look for a library map or shelving plan to tell you where your book is housed. Whether or not you find your book, take the time to browse through the books nearby. Very often you will find the area where your book belongs a more important treasure trove than any bibliography or index.

If the computer tells you that the book is checked out or if your book is not on the shelf, ask about it at the circulation desk. The book may not circulate, or it may be in an area closed to the public. If someone has checked it out, the library might recall it for you. Consider your deadline, and determine whether it is realistic to request a recall.

Indexes to Books and Reviews

Book indexes can be helpful for quickly locating complete information on a book when you know only one piece of it—the author's last name, perhaps, or the title. These sources can also be valuable for alerting you to other works by a particular author or on a particular subject. Note that such indexes are available either online or on CD-ROM.

Books in Print. 1948–; annual. Lists by author, subject, and title all books distributed in the United States that are currently in print. (online by subscription, CD-ROM)

Cumulative Book Index. 1898–; monthly. Lists by author, subject, and title books in English distributed in the United States and internationally. (online by subscription, CD-ROM)

Paperbound Books in Print. 1955–; semiannual. Lists by author, subject, and title all paperback books distributed in the United States that are currently in print. (CD-ROM)

Consider also using a review index to check the relevance of a source or to get a thumbnail sketch of its contents. Be sure to check not only the year of a book's publication but also the next year.

Book Review Digest. 1905–; annual. Contains excerpts from reviews of books along with information for locating the full reviews in popular and scholarly periodicals. (online by subscription, CD-ROM, 1983–)

Book Review Index. 1965–; annual. Identifies dates and locations for finding full reviews in several hundred popular and scholarly periodicals; organizes entries by the name of the book's author.

Look also for specialized review indexes such as the *Index to Book Reviews in the Humanities* or the *Index to Book Reviews in the Social Sciences.*

Indexes to Newspapers, Magazines, and Journals

Periodical indexes are guides to articles published in newspapers, magazines, and scholarly journals, items that will not appear in your library's catalog. Each index covers a specific group of periodicals, usually identified at the beginning of the index or volume. In addition to printed indexes, your library will have indexes on CD-ROM, online, or on microform. Microforms are rolls (microfilm) or sheets (microfiche) of film that must be read on special machines. Ask the librarian for help in locating microforms and using the machines. Microform indexes cover only the past three or four years, so if you are searching for earlier material, check the printed or electronic indexes.

GENERAL INDEXES

General indexes of periodicals list articles from current general-interest magazines (such as *Time* and *Newsweek*), newspapers, or a combination of these. General indexes will usually provide current sources on your topic, though they may not treat the topic in sufficient depth for your purposes.

Access: The Supplementary Index. 1979–; monthly. Indexes magazines not covered by the *Readers' Guide to Periodical Literature* (see below), such as regional and particular-interest magazines (the environment, women's issues).

Alternative Press Index. 1970–; monthly. Indexes alternative and radical publications.

InfoTrac. Updated monthly. Includes three indexes: (1) the *General Periodicals Index* (current year and past four years), which covers over eleven hundred general-interest publications, incorporating the *Magazine Index* and including the *New York Times* and *Wall Street Journal;* (2) the *Academic Index* (current year and past four years), which covers over nine hundred scholarly and general-interest publications, including the *New York Times;* and (3) the *National Newspaper Index* (current year and past three years). Some entries include a summary or even the entire article. (online by subscription, CD-ROM)

Magazine Index. Updated monthly. Analyzes over five hundred general-interest magazines. Available on microfilm (1988–), online by subscription (1973–), and on CD-ROM, separately and as part of InfoTrac (see above).

National Newspaper Index. Updated monthly. Covers the *New York Times, Los Angeles Times, Wall Street Journal, Washington Post,* and *Christian Science Monitor.* Available on microfilm (1989–), online by subscription (1979–), and on CD-ROM, separately and as part of InfoTrac (see above).

NewsBank. 1970–; updated monthly. Includes over one million articles from five hundred U.S. newspapers. Available on microfiche, online by subscription, and on CD-ROM.

Newspaper Abstracts Ondisc. 1985–. Contains abstracts from eight major newspapers, updated monthly. (online by subscription, CD-ROM)

New York Times Index. 1851–; bimonthly with annual cumulations. Lists by subject every article that has appeared in the *New York Times.* For most articles of any length, short summaries are given as well. Also available online through NEXIS (1980–; see below).

LEXIS/NEXIS. 1974–. LEXIS contains legal, legislative, and regulatory information. NEXIS contains full texts and abstracts of newspapers, magazines, wire services, newsletters, company and industry analyst reports, and broadcast transcripts. (online by subscription)

Nineteenth Century Readers' Guide to Periodical Literature. 1890–99. (See also *Readers' Guide,* below.)

Periodical Abstracts Ondisc. 1986–. Contains abstracts of articles in over one thousand periodicals and journals in science, social science, humanities, and business. (online by subscription, CD-ROM)

Poole's Index to Periodical Literature. 1802–1907. Indexes nineteenth-century British and American periodicals.

Readers' Guide to Periodical Literature. 1900–; semimonthly with quarterly and annual cumulations. Indexes articles from over 170 magazines. Particularly helpful for social trends, popular scientific questions, and contemporary political issues. Entries are arranged by author and subject with cross-references leading to related topics. (online by subscription, CD-ROM)

Times Index (London). 1913–; bimonthly. Lists articles and summaries of stories published in the London *Times.*

SPECIALIZED INDEXES AND ABSTRACTS

Many disciplines have specialized indexes and abstracts to help researchers find detailed information. In general, such works list articles in scholarly journals for that discipline, but they may include other publications as well; check the beginning of the index or the volume. For more information on specialized indexes and abstracts in particular fields, see Chapters 5–8. To use these resources most efficiently, ask a reference librarian to help you identify those most likely to address your topic. Page 31 shows an example of the results from a search of the specialized electronic index ERIC.

LOCATING INDEXED ARTICLES

To locate an indexed article that seems promising for your research project you can check the Web and the online library catalog to see whether the periodical is available electronically and, if so, whether your library offers access to it. By using the library computer network for access, you can often avoid subscription charges or fees for viewing the text of an article. For example, the *New York Times* on the Web, <www.nytimes.com>, a very useful source for many topics currently in the news, charges three dollars to view or download most articles that are more than a week old.

If the periodical is not available electronically (as many scholarly journals, for example, are not), if your library does not offer free access to it through a database, or if you simply prefer to look at a print version, the library catalog will tell you whether one is available in the library's periodicals room. This room will probably have recent issues of hundreds or even thousands of newspapers, magazines, and journals, and it may also contain bound volumes of past issues and microfilm copies of older newspapers. (The *New York Times,* for example, is most likely available in your library on microfilm.)

Bibliographies

Finding good bibliographies (lists of sources) can speed up your research, so it is well worth your time to consider them. Look at any bibliographies in books or articles you are using for your research; they can lead you to other valuable resources. In addition, check with

ERIC Accessed via CSA Internet Database Service

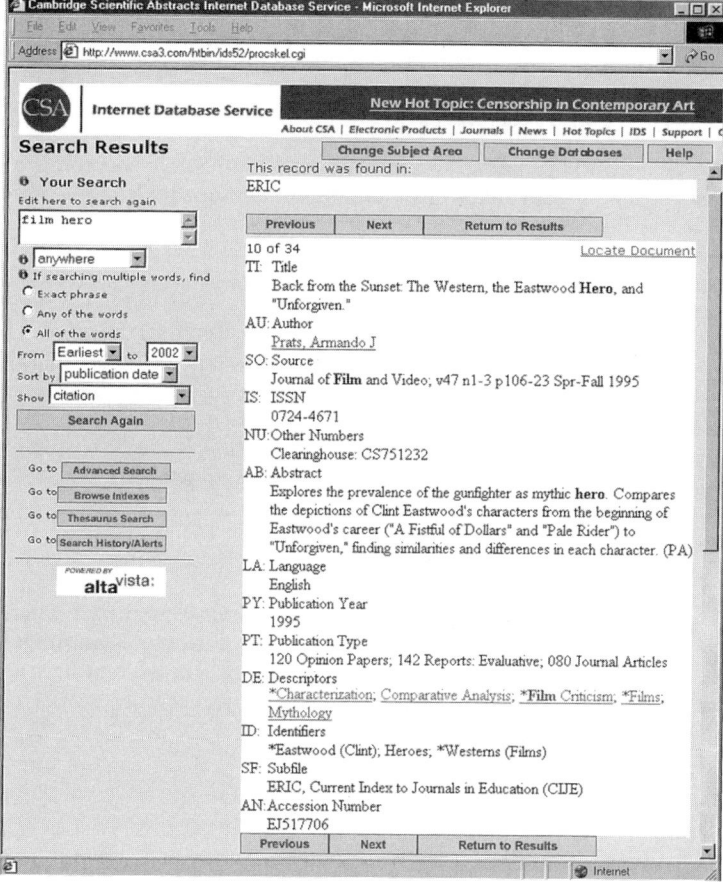

your reference librarian to find out whether the library has more extensive bibliographies devoted to the area of your research. At one time, all such bibliographies were bound in printed volumes; increasingly, however, these resources are available online.

Other Library Resources

In addition to books and periodicals, libraries give you access to many other useful materials that might be appropriate for your research.

SPECIAL COLLECTIONS AND ARCHIVES

Your library will probably have one area, often referred to as *special collections,* devoted to rare books and manuscripts. In this area or elsewhere, your library may house archives, collections of valuable papers and related materials, that could be helpful to you in your research. Special collections and archives are often available to undergraduate students, so ask your reference librarian whether they contain possible sources on your topic.

AUDIO, VIDEO, AND ART COLLECTIONS

Many academic libraries include an area devoted to media, where they collect films and videos as well as sound recordings. Your library may also have a section devoted to art collections—or you may have an art museum on campus that will give you access to primary works for your research.

GOVERNMENT DOCUMENTS AND STATISTICAL SOURCES

You can use the library's or your own networked computer to check the online version of the *Catalog of U.S. Government Publications,* <www.access.gpo.gov/su_docs/locators/cgp/index.html>, to identify publications appropriate to your topic and then see if your library has them. For statistical information, consult the sources on page 19, and ask your reference librarian to recommend more specialized statistical sources you might need. *The Gallup Poll,* for example, provides public opinion statistics, and the *Dow Jones–Irwin Business Almanac* offers business data.

INTERLIBRARY LOANS

Your library can often arrange for you to borrow books, journals, and video or audio materials from another library. Such loans can take time, however, and may involve some cost to you, so make sure you really need the source and can get it in time to make good use of it.

Using the Web

The World Wide Web is many college students' favorite resource for accessing information. But since anyone can post a document to the Web and no one is responsible for regulating the staggering number of texts and sites, it's possible to find anything there, from the most ridiculous statements to outright misinformation, lies, and libel. As a result, you need to use information from the Web with great care.

Search Tools

Browsers such as Netscape Navigator and Internet Explorer give you access to powerful search engines and subject directories that allow you to carry out research online. Clicking on SEARCH takes you to the search tools programmed into your browser, but you're free to use others as well.

Most search tools allow keyword searches as well as subject directory or category searches. If you're using a search engine, you simply type in keywords and get results; some metasearch tools use several search engines at once and compile their findings. In a subject directory, on the other hand, the first screen lists a number of categories you can click on to begin your search, which you can then narrow by clicking on increasingly specific subcategories. For example, in the Yahoo! subject directory, you can click on "Entertainment" if you are working on a research project in that area, and then click on "Movies and Film" and then "Theory and Criticism." Each click narrows and focuses your search. At any point, you can switch to a keyword search to look for specific terms and topics.

Here is a list of some of the most-often-used search tools.

SEARCH TOOLS

AlltheWeb <www.alltheweb.com> allows keyword searches and has sophisticated advanced search options.

AltaVista <www.altavista.digital.com> lets you search the entire Web using either a single Keyword or multiple keywords.

Excite <www.excite.com> allows you to do keyword and subject directory searches.

Google <www.google.com> is a popular search tool that is a favorite of many students. keyword and subject directory searches.

HotBot <www.hotbot.com> lets you search using one of several search engines and to narrow the search to specific dates, media, and other criteria. Allows keyword and subject directory searches.

Lycos <www.lycos.com> allows you to search a huge catalog of Web sites and includes multimedia documents. Keyword and subject directory searches.

Teoma <www.teoma.com> is a search engine that ranks a result's relevance based on the number of same-subject pages that refer to it, not just general popularity.

(Continued)

> *Yahoo!* <www.yahoo.com> allows you either to search directories of sites related to particular subjects (such as entertainment or education) or to enter keywords that Yahoo! gives to a search engine, which sends back the results.
>
> **Metasearch Tools**
>
> *Ixquick* <www.ixquick.com> is a speedy metasearch tool that allows you to search fourteen other engines or directories at the same time using keywords.
>
> *ProFusion* <www.profusion.com> is another metasearch tool.
>
> *WebCrawler* <www.webcrawler.com> searches using several engines (including some that return sponsored listings) and subject directories.
>
> *Zworks* <www.zworks.com> calls itself "the metasearch loved by parents and webmasters alike" because it can be filtered. Also ranks results for relevancy.

Keywords, Boolean Operators, and Quotation Marks

Since different search tools have different rules for using keywords, it's best to read the FAQ (frequently asked questions), information, or help section of the search tool you are using carefully. Also, be careful to make your keywords as narrow as possible. If you are interested in legal issues regarding the Internet, for example, and you enter *Internet* and *law* as keywords in a search on Google, you will get over three million possible sources. The keywords you choose—names, titles, authors, concepts—need to lead you to more specific sources. In this case, entering the name of a well-known legal theorist, *Lawrence Lessig,* along with another keyword, *speeches,* returns about two hundred responses, which is a much more reasonable number to consider.

To search using more than one keyword at a time, it's helpful to use your search tool's advanced-search options. Most search engines now offer these options (sometimes on a separate advanced-search page) to help you easily combine keywords, search for an exact phrase, or exclude items containing particular keywords; often they let you limit your search in other ways as well, such as by date, language, country of origin, or location of the keyword within a site. On page 37, for example, is an advanced search within Yahoo! using the exact phrase *film hero* together with the keyword *cyborg* and limited to pages in English updated in the past year. This search yielded twelve listings; the first page of the search results is shown on page 38.

With many search engines, you can also use quotation marks to create an exact phrase for your search. In addition, many library catalogs and some search engines offer a search option using the Boolean operators AND, NOT, and OR, as well as parentheses and quotation marks. The Boolean operators work this way:

HOLLYWOOD AND *HEROES*

AND *limits your search.* If you enter the terms *Hollywood* AND *heroes*, the search engine will retrieve *only* those items that contain *both* those terms. The following diagram shows how this operator works (the items retrieved using AND are shaded dark):

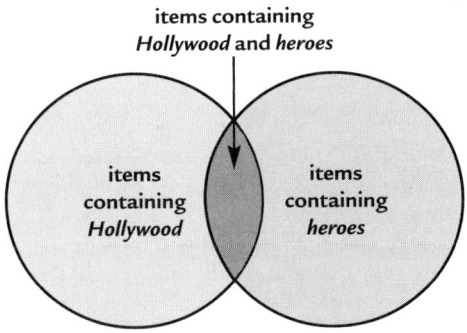

Using the Web 37

Yahoo! Advanced Search

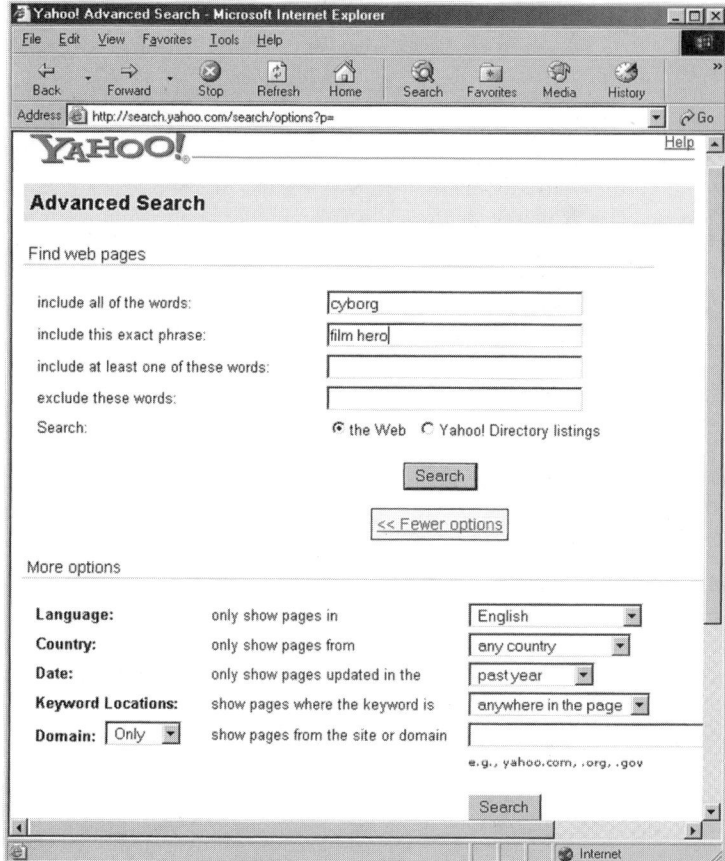

Sample Yahoo! Search Results

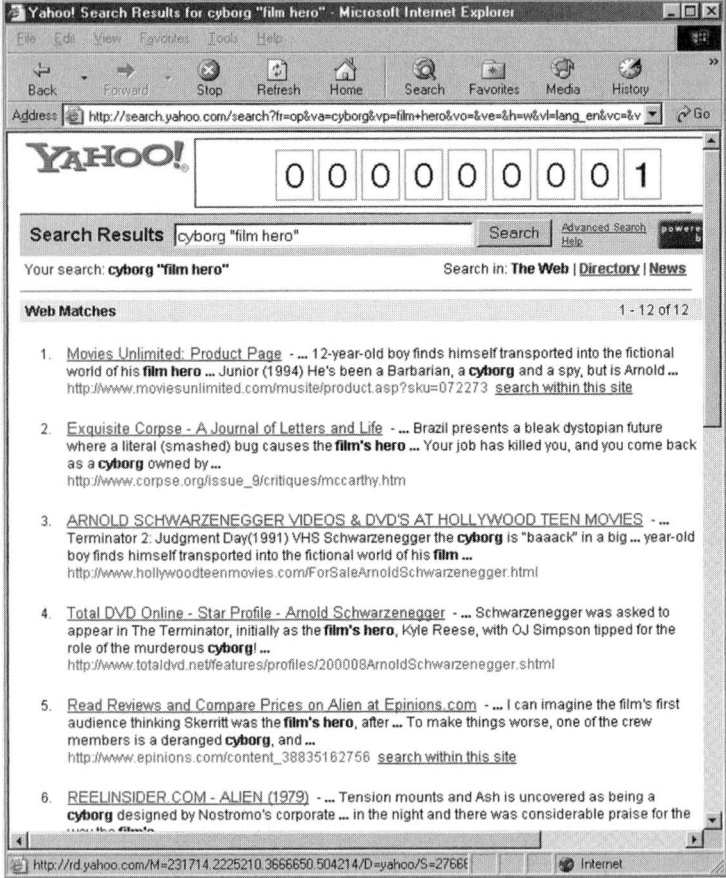

HOLLYWOOD NOT HEROES

NOT *also limits your search.* If you enter the terms *Hollywood NOT heroes,* the search engine will retrieve every item that contains *Holly-*

wood except those that also contain the term *heroes*. The following diagram shows how NOT works (the items retrieved using NOT are shaded dark):

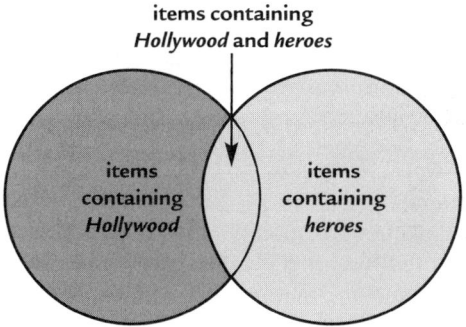

HOLLYWOOD OR HEROES

OR *expands your search*. If you enter the terms *Hollywood OR heroes*, the computer will retrieve every item that contains the term *Hollywood* and every item that contains the term *heroes*. In this case, the OR stands for MORE, since you will probably get many more sources using OR than you would by entering either term alone. The following diagram shows how OR works (the items retrieved using OR are shaded dark):

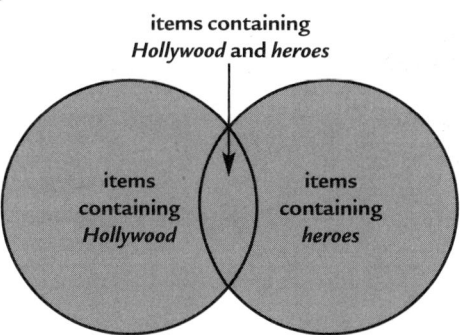

Parentheses can customize your search still further. Entering *Oscar AND (Denzel Washington OR Will Smith),* for example, will locate items that mention either of those actors in connection with the Academy Awards, while entering *film NOT (western OR thriller)* will exclude those kinds of films from your search. Quotation marks around a phrase can also help you narrow your search because they indicate that all the words in the phrase must appear together in the exact order you have typed them. This option is especially important because some search engines assume that when multiple keywords are entered, AND is between them. When the keywords *Hollywood movie heroes* were typed in for a search on Google, it yielded 140,000 hits. But when the three terms were put in one set of quotation marks, Google returned only six sources. (Search engines generally recognize proper names like *George Bush* or *New York* as a unit, however, so you don't need to use quotation marks around them.)

In general, type the Boolean operators in capital letters. Some search engines use symbols instead of words: the plus sign (+) or ampersand (&) for AND, the minus sign or hyphen (-) for NOT, and the | sign for OR (located on the backslash key on most keyboards). To save time (and maybe money), make sure you understand the rules for a particular search engine before you begin using it.

Online Libraries, Governmental and News Sites, and Periodicals

Today, students have online access to some information in libraries other than their own. These virtual libraries are sites on the Internet that allow you access to some of another library's collection. The University of California at Berkeley, for example, has a site, <www.sunsite.berkeley.edu>, that allows students at other institutions to access its digital collections of documents and images.

Other online collections you may find helpful are housed in governmental sites.

Bureau of Labor Statistics <www.bls.gov> provides information by region. Allows you to search by keyword.

Library of Congress <www.lcweb.loc.gov> offers a vast array of information, including legislative information, information on copyright and intellectual property, and collections such as American Memory, which contains more than seven million digital items from over a hundred historical collections. Allows searches by title, author/creator, subject, or keyword.

National Institutes of Health <www.nih.gov> provides data on health and medical issues. Allows keyword searches.

Statistical Abstracts of the United States <www.census.gov/statab/www> provides information on social and economic trends. Allows searches by keyword or place.

U.S. Census Bureau <www.census.gov> provides data on population and other demographic data. Allows you to search by keyword, place, or region.

For current news events, you can consult online versions of newspapers such as the *New York Times* at <www.nytimes.com> or the *Chicago Tribune* at <www.chicagotribune.com>. CNN at <www.cnn.com> and C-SPAN at <www.c-span.org> are among the many other newspapers and news services available electronically. You can also use a search tool like Yahoo!, which has a "News and Media" category you can click on the main page, <www.yahoo.com>, or you can check daily news at <www.dailynews.yahoo.com>.

Some scholarly journals and at least two general-interest magazines, *Slate* at <www.slate.com> and *Salon* at <www.salon.com>, are now published only on the Web, and many other journals and magazines including *Newsweek,* the *New Yorker,* and the *New Republic* make at least part of their contents available online. In many cases, as noted earlier, a paid subscription or a one-time fee is required to view or download articles, but you may be able to avoid these charges by using the library's computers. To access a wide variety of online articles from many different magazines, try the Web sites <www.elibrary.com> and <www.newsdirectory.com>.

Reference Sources about the Internet and the World Wide Web

For more information and detailed help on navigating the Internet and the Web, check out Andrew Harnack and Eugene Kleppinger's *Online! A Reference Guide to Using Internet Sources.* An online version is also available:

<http://www.bedfordstmartins.com/online/>

Two other helpful online sources focus on how to use different search engines and browser capabilities:

<http://daphne.palomar.edu/TGSEARCH/>
<http://lib.berkeley.edu/TeachingLib/Guides/Internet/FindInfo.html>

Print sources of information about working online include the following:

Cadenhead, Rogers. *How to Use the Internet.* 8th ed. Indianapolis: Que, 2002.

Krol, Ed. *The Whole Internet User's Guide & Catalog.* Sebastopol: O'Reilly & Associates, 1996.

Li, Xia, and Nancy B. Crane. *Electronic Style: A Guide to Citing Electronic Information.* Westport: Meckler, 1996.

The following general Web sites provide access to a wide range of information and more specialized sites.

American Library Association: Links to Library Web Resources
<http://www.ala.org/library/weblinks.html>
Supplies links to notable library-related organizations and resources.

Infomine: Scholarly Internet Resource Collections
<http://infomine.ucr.edu>
Supplies indexed and annotated links to more than 9,500 databases and other resources of academic interest, grouped in interdisciplinary categories; also includes resources on using the Internet, maps, and teaching materials.

The Internet Public Library
<http://www.ipl.org>
Selects worthwhile sources and organizes information by subject category; a highly recommended site with many references, exhibits, and useful resources.

Librarians' Index to the Internet
<http://lii.org>
Includes general reference information, topics of popular interest (as varied as automobiles, food, government, health, music, and recreation), and subjects ranging from the arts to world cultures.

The Library of Congress World Wide Web HomePage
<http://lcweb.loc.gov>
Provides links to information on all Internet sources.

My Virtual Reference Desk
<http://www.refdesk.com>
Supplies access to reference materials, a variety of news organizations, and sites related to topics of current interest.

News Index
<http://www.newsindex.com>
Provides topic searches and access to the Web sites of 250 newspapers and periodicals.

UniGuide Academic Guide to the Internet
<http://www.aldea.com/guides/ag/attframes2.html>
Offers academic links in disciplines from the biological sciences to liberal arts.

The Webliography: Internet Subject Guides
<http://www.lib.lsu.edu/weblio.html>
Provides extensive annotated guides and access to academic and government resources in the humanities, sciences, and social sciences.

WWW Virtual Library
<http://www.vlib.org>
Provides links to Library of Congress topics.

3
Evaluating Sources and Taking Notes

Evaluating Potential Sources for Usefulness and Credibility

Since you want the information and other ideas you glean from sources to be reliable and persuasive, you must evaluate each potential source carefully.

- *What is your purpose in using the source?* Does it help you support a major point; demonstrate that you have thoroughly reviewed the literature on your topic; help establish your own credibility through its authority? If you can't think of a good reason for using the source, put it aside; you can always come back to it later on if you decide it might be useful.
- *How closely related is the source to the narrowed and focused topic you are pursuing?* You may need to read beyond the title and opening paragraph to check for relevance.
- *What are the credentials of the publisher or sponsor?* For example, is it an article from a popular magazine such as *People*, or from a journal sponsored by a professional or scholarly organization such as the *Journal of the American Medical Association*? No hard-and-fast rules exist for deciding what credentials are most appropriate. You may have very good reason to use information from a popular magazine, but

remember that scholarly journals carry greater authority because of their professional or academic sponsors.

Online, there may be a huge difference between the credibility of a page posted by an individual and that of a Web site sponsored by an academic institution or a nonprofit organization. The domain types that come after the "dot" in a URL can tell you something about the sponsor:

.edu—education-sponsored site

.gov—government-sponsored site

.mil—military-sponsored site

.org—nonprofit organization–sponsored site

.net—network-sponsored site

.com—commercially sponsored site

You can also tell whether the site originates in another country: .ca indicates Canada; .mx, Mexico; .uk, the United Kingdom; .au, Australia; and so on.

- *What are the credentials of the author?* Note authors' names that keep coming up from one source to another, since these references may indicate that the author is well known or influential in the field. The author's credentials may be presented in the article, book, or Web site itself, or you can go to the Internet to gather information about an author: just open a search tool and type in the name, or search Google/Groups for postings that mention the author.
- *What is the date of publication, posting, or updating?* If you are researching how Shakespeare's *Othello* was reviewed in performances immediately after the Civil War, you will need to rely on sources over a century old. On the other hand, if you are working on research related to a current medical development, access to the most recent information is very important.
- *How accurate and complete is the information the source contains?* While you often will not have the knowledge to judge its full accuracy, can you find other sources that corroborate what it is saying?
- *What is the stance or point of view of the source,* and what does the author or sponsor want to make happen: convince you of an idea? sell you something? call you to action in some way?

- *Are there cross-references to the source in other sources?* If you see your source cited by others, looking at how they cite it and what they say about it can provide additional clues to its credibility. So take a look at the bibliographies of all the sources you are using, and see what cross-references you can find.

As you evaluate the usefulness and credibility of potential sources, it is helpful to look quickly at the parts of a source that are listed in the guidelines box below. If you decide you want to explore a particular source more thoroughly, these elements can also help you read critically.

SOME GUIDELINES FOR EXAMINING POTENTIAL SOURCES

- *Title and subtitle.* If you are researching coeducation in the nineteenth century and find a book called *Women in Education,* the subtitle *The Challenge of the 1970s* will tell you that you probably don't need to examine the book.
- *Title page and copyright page.* In a book, these pages will show you when the book was originally published, whether it is a revised edition, and who published it.
- *Abstract.* Concise summaries of articles or books, abstracts routinely precede articles in some journals and are included in some periodical or bibliographic guides. They can help you decide whether to read the entire work.
- *Table of contents.* Part and chapter titles can help you determine whether the chapter topics are specific enough to be useful. In a periodical, the table of contents often includes brief descriptions of articles.
- *Preface or foreword.* This often details the writer's purposes, range of interests, intended audience, topic restrictions, research limitations, and thesis.

(Continued)

- *Subheadings.* Subheadings in the text can give you an idea of how much detail is given on a topic and whether that detail would be helpful to you.
- *Conclusion or afterword.* This summary could help you decide how appropriate that source is for your project.
- *Note on the author.* Check the dust jacket of a book, the first and last few pages of a work, or an article itself for information about the author.
- *Index.* Check the index for words and topics key to your project. Are the listings for your key terms many or few?
- *Bibliography and/or footnotes.* Lists of references show how carefully a writer has investigated the subject. They may also help you find other sources.

Extra Considerations for Electronic Sources

- *Home- or first page.* This page should tell you about the sponsorship of the source, letting you know who can be held accountable for the information in it. (Sometimes you will need to click on an "About Us" or "About Me" button to learn about the sponsor.) Can you determine the goal of the document or site—to provide information, to express an opinion, to get you to sign up for or buy something?
- *Links.* The links help you learn how credible and useful the source is. Click on some of them, if necessary, to see if they lead to legitimate and helpful sites.
- *Design.* The design of the document or site may give you clues to the usefulness of the information it provides. How user-friendly is it? Is it easy to navigate?
- *Bulletin boards or newsgroup discussions.* Be wary of these sources, which at their best can spark ideas or lead you to investigate an aspect of your topic. Contributors are not likely to be credible experts.

Reading Sources with a Critical Eye

Because of time constraints and the wealth of material available on most topics, you probably will not have time to read through all of your potential material. For those sources that you do want to analyze more closely, however, reading with a critical eye can make your research process more efficient. The following considerations can guide your critical reading:

Reading with Your Research Question in Mind

- How does this material address your research question?
- In what ways does it provide support for your hypothesis?
- What quotations from this source might help support your hypothesis?
- Does the source include counterarguments to your hypothesis that you will need to answer? If so, what answers can you provide?

Analyzing the Author's Stance and Tone

- Is the author an enthusiastic advocate of something, a strong opponent, a skeptical critic, an amused onlooker, a confident specialist in the field? Are there any clues to why the author takes this stance? What forces in society may have shaped or influenced it?
- How does this stance affect the author's presentation?
- If the author has a professional affiliation, how might the affiliation affect his or her stance?
- In what ways do you share—or not share—the author's stance?
- What is the author's tone? Is it cautious, angry, flippant, serious, impassioned? What words express this tone?

Assessing the Author's Argument and Evidence

- What is the author's main point?
- How much and what kind of evidence supports that point?
- How persuasive do you find the evidence?
- Can you offer counterarguments to or refutations of the evidence?
- Can you detect any questionable logic or fallacious thinking?

Questioning Your Sources

Because all sources make an explicit or implicit argument, they often disagree with one another. Disagreements among sources arise sometimes from differences about facts, sometimes from differences about how to interpret facts. For instance, if an authoritative source says that the chances of a nuclear power plant melting down are 1 in 100,000, commentators could interpret that statistic very differently. A critic of nuclear power could argue that nuclear accidents are so terrible that this chance is too great to take, while a supporter of nuclear power could argue that such a small chance is essentially no chance at all.

The point is that all knowledge is interpreted subjectively. A writer may well tell nothing but the truth, but he or she can never tell the *whole* truth because people are not all-knowing. Thus you must examine all sources critically, using them not as unquestioned authorities but as contributions to your own informed opinion, your own truth.

Interpreting Sources: Synthesizing Data and Drawing Inferences

Your task as a reader is to identify and understand sources and sets of data as completely as possible. As a writer, your aim must be to present data and sources *to other readers* so that they can readily understand the point you are making. Doing so calls for you to notice patterns in your sources and to develop your own interpretation of them.

Throughout the research process, you are synthesizing—grouping similar pieces of data together, looking for patterns or trends, and identifying the gist, or main points, of the data. Doing so enables you to use your sources in pursuit of your own goals, rather than just stacking them up as unconnected bits of information. Often such synthesizing will lead you to make inferences—conclusions that are not explicitly stated in but that follow logically from the data given.

TAKING ACCURATE NOTES

- Using a computer file, index cards, or a notebook, list the author's name and a shortened title of the source for each note. Your working-bibliography entry for the source should contain full publication information, so you don't need to repeat it in the note. If you are combining your working bibliography with your notes, however, be sure to take down all the information you will need before beginning on the notes.
- Record exact page references. If the note refers to more than one page, indicate page breaks so that if you decide to use only part of the note, you will know which page to cite. For online sources without page numbers, record the paragraph, screen, or other section number(s) if indicated.
- Label each note with a subject heading or category so you can group similar subtopics together.
- Identify the note as a quotation, a paraphrase, a summary, a combination of these forms, or some other form—such as your own critical comment—to avoid any confusion later. Mark quotations accurately with quotation marks, and paraphrase and summarize completely in your own words to be sure you do not inadvertently plagiarize the source.
- Read over each completed note carefully to recheck the accuracy of quotations, statistics, and specific facts.

TAKING QUOTATION NOTES

- Copy quotations *carefully,* with punctuation, capitalization, and spelling exactly as in the original.
- Use square brackets if you introduce words of your own into a quotation or make changes in it, and use ellipses if you omit material. If you later incorporate the quotation into your essay, copy it faithfully—brackets, ellipses, and all.
- It is especially important to enclose the quotation in quotation marks; don't rely on your memory to distinguish your own words from those of the source.
- Record the author's name, shortened title, and page number(s) on which the quotation appeared. For online sources without page numbers, record the paragraph, screen, or other section number(s) if indicated.
- Make sure you have a corresponding working-bibliography entry with complete source information.
- Label the note with a subject heading.

TAKING PARAPHRASE NOTES

- Include all main points and any important details from the original, in the same order in which they were presented.
- State the meaning in your own words and sentence structures. If you want to include especially memorable language from the original, enclose it in quotation marks.
- Leave out your own comments, elaborations, or reactions.

(Continued)

- Record the author, shortened title, and page number(s) on which the original material appeared. For online sources without page numbers, record the paragraph, screen, or other section number(s) if indicated.
- Make sure you have a corresponding working-bibliography entry with complete source information.
- Label the note with a subject heading, and identify it as a paraphrase to avoid confusion with a summary.
- Recheck to be sure that the words and sentence structures are your own and that they express the author's meaning accurately.

TAKING SUMMARY NOTES

- Include just enough information to recount the main points you wish to cite. A summary is usually far shorter than the original.
- Use your own words. If you include language from the original, enclose it in quotation marks.
- Record the author, shortened title, and page number(s) on which the original material appeared. For online sources without page numbers, record the paragraph, screen, or other section number(s) if indicated.
- Make sure you have a corresponding working-bibliography entry with complete source information.
- Label the note with a subject heading, and identify it as a summary to avoid confusion with a paraphrase.
- Recheck to be sure you have captured the author's meaning and that the words are entirely your own.

KNOWING WHEN TO QUOTE, PARAPHRASE, OR SUMMARIZE

QUOTE

- wording that is so memorable or powerful or expresses a point so perfectly that you cannot change it without weakening the meaning you need
- authors' opinions you wish to emphasize
- authors' words that show you are considering varying perspectives
- respected authorities whose opinions support your ideas
- authors whose opinions challenge or vary greatly from those of others in the field

PARAPHRASE

- passages you do not wish to quote but whose details are important to your point

SUMMARIZE

- long passages whose main point is important to your point but whose details are not

4

Acknowledging Sources and Avoiding Plagiarism

Which Sources to Acknowledge

As you carry out research, it is important to understand the distinction between materials that require acknowledgment and those that do not.

Materials That Don't Require Acknowledgment

Some of the information you use does not need to be credited to a source because it is well known or because you gathered the data yourself.

- *Common knowledge.* If most readers already know a fact, you probably do not need to cite a source for it. You do not need to credit a source for the statement that George Bush was elected president in 2000, for example. If, on the other hand, you are discussing the very close nature of the election and offering various experts' opinions on the outcome, you should cite the sources of that information.
- *Facts available in a wide variety of sources.* If a number of encyclopedias, almanacs, or textbooks include a certain piece of information, you usually need not cite a specific source for it. For instance, you would not need to cite a source for the fact that the Japanese bombing of

Pearl Harbor on December 7, 1941, destroyed most of the base except for the oil tanks and submarines. You would, however, need to credit a source that argued that the failure to destroy the submarines meant that Japan was destined to lose the subsequent war with the United States.

- *Visuals you created yourself.* If you took the photograph or drew the diagram, you do not need to cite yourself as the source. If you used information from a source to create a visual such as a table, chart, or graph, however, credit the source of the information.
- *Your own findings from field research.* If you conduct observations or surveys, simply announce your findings as your own. Do acknowledge people you interview as individuals rather than as part of a survey, however.

When you are not sure whether a fact, an observation, or a piece of information requires acknowledgment, err on the side of safety and cite the source.

Materials That Require Acknowledgment

For material that does not fall under the preceding categories, credit sources as fully as possible. Using quotation marks where appropriate, follow the conventions of the citation style you are using (such as MLA or APA), and include each source in a bibliography or list of works cited.

- *Direct quotations.* Whenever you use another person's words directly, credit the source. If two quotations from the same source appear close together, you can use one parenthetical reference, or note, after the second quotation to refer to both. If you quote some of an author's words within a paraphrase or summary, you need to include a parenthetical reference for the quotation separately, after the closing quotation mark, as one student did when she quoted from Philip G. Hamerton's "One Intellectual Life":

    Writer Philip G. Hamerton makes an interesting point about quotation when he says that readers "pay much more attention to a wise passage when it is quoted by someone else" (42).

- *Facts that aren't widely known or claims that are arguable.* If your readers would be unlikely to know a fact, or if an author presents as fact a claim that may or may not be true, cite the source. To claim, for instance, that Switzerland is amassing an offensive nuclear arsenal would demand the citation of a source because Switzerland has long been an officially neutral state. If you are not sure whether a fact will be familiar to your readers or whether a statement is arguable, go ahead and cite the source.
- *Judgments and opinions of others.* Whenever you summarize or paraphrase someone else's ideas or opinions, give the source on which you based your summary or paraphrase. Even though the wording is completely your own, you should acknowledge your source.
- *Images, statistics, charts, tables, graphs, and other visuals from any source.* Credit all visual and statistical material not derived from your own field research, even if you yourself create a graph or table from the data provided in a source.
- *Help provided by friends, instructors, and others.* A conference with an instructor may give you the perfect idea for clinching an argument. If so, give credit. Friends may respond to your drafts or help you conduct surveys. Credit them, too.

Here is a quick-reference chart to guide you in deciding whether you need to acknowledge a source:

NEED TO ACKNOWLEDGE

quotations
summaries or paraphrases of a source
ideas you glean from a source
facts that aren't widely known
graphs, tables, and other statistical information taken or derived from a source
photographs, illustrations, or other visuals you do not create
experiments conducted by others
opinions and judgments of others
interviews that are not part of a survey
video or sound taken from sources
organization or structure taken from a source

DON'T NEED TO ACKNOWLEDGE

your own words, observations, surveys, and so on
common knowledge
facts available in many sources
graphs or tables you create from statistics you compile on your own
drawings you create

Academic Integrity and Plagiarism

One of the cornerstones of intellectual work is academic integrity. This principle accounts for our being able to trust those sources we use and to demonstrate that our own work is equally trustworthy. While there are many ways to damage academic integrity, two that are especially important are inaccurate or incomplete citation of sources—sometimes called *unintentional plagiarism*—and plagiarism that is deliberately intended to pass off one writer's work as another's.

Inaccurate or Incomplete Citation of Sources

If you use a paraphrase that is too close to the original wording or sentence structure (even if you include a parenthetical reference, or note), if you leave out the parenthetical reference for a quotation (even if you include the quotation marks), or if you fail to indicate clearly the source of an idea that you obviously did not come up with on your own, you may be accused of plagiarism even if your intent was not to plagiarize. This kind of inaccurate or incomplete citation of sources often results either from carelessness or from not learning how to use citations accurately and fully. Still, because the costs of even unintentional plagiarism can be severe, it's important to understand how it can happen and how you can guard against it.

As a writer of academic integrity, you will want to take responsibility for your research and for citing all sources accurately. Doing so is considerably easier now, when sources can be photocopied and the needed quotations identified right on the copy, and when software programs allow writers to insert footnotes or endnotes into the text as they are writing it.

Intentional Plagiarism

Deliberate plagiarism—handing in an essay written by a friend or purchased (or simply downloaded) from an essay-writing company; cutting and pasting passages directly from source materials without marking them with quotation marks and citing sources for them; failing to credit the source of an idea or concept in your text—is what most people think of when they hear the word *plagiarism.*

This form of plagiarism is particularly troubling because it represents dishonesty and deception: those who intentionally plagiarize present the hard thinking and hard work of someone else as their own, and they claim knowledge they really don't have, thus deceiving their readers. You are probably already convinced that such deception can lead to disaster: how many of us would want to be operated on by a doctor who plagiarized her way through medical school or represented by a lawyer who cheated his way through law school—or drive over bridges engineered by those who downloaded answers to engineering problems, never working out the problems for themselves?

Intentional plagiarism is also fairly simple to spot: your instructor will be very well acquainted with your writing and likely to notice any sudden shifts in the style or quality of your work. In addition, by typing a few words into <www.google.com>, your instructor can identify "matches" very easily.

Tips for Using Sources

Precisely because downloading material from the Web and cutting and pasting from one document to another are so simple today, you need to be even more careful about the sources you work with. Instructor Nick Carbone provides the following advice for students who are working with sources in their writing:

Academic Integrity and Plagiarism

DO

- Share ideas with others, give and get responses to writing, help one another write.
- Edit sections of one another's papers from time to time.
- Expect to make mistakes in managing and citing your sources.
- Expect to correct such mistakes.
- Be careful in downloading sources and in taking notes.
- Find a way to use your sources fairly and wisely, without these sources taking over your essay.
- Learn the many purposes that using and citing sources can have in your writing.
- Use your word processor to help you manage sources (for example, put sources you're quoting or paraphrasing in a different font and font color until your final draft so you don't forget they came from one of your sources).
- See your instructor when you are in doubt about how to use or acknowledge a source.
- Tell your instructor if you feel overwhelmed or fall behind; knowing your predicament will enable the instructor to help you find a solution.

DON'T

- Don't cheat, steal, or misrepresent the work of others as your own.
- Don't use online term-paper mills; they aren't worthy of you.
- Don't think that because something is on the Net it doesn't need to be acknowledged in a citation.
- Don't think that simply changing a few words means you don't have to provide a citation and put what is quoted in quotation marks.
- Don't think that because politicians have speechwriters whom they don't acknowledge you can reasonably get someone else to write a paper for you: the purpose of being in college is to acquire knowledge through your own research and writing.
- Don't procrastinate on assignments so that you put undue pressure on yourself and are tempted to take shortcuts.

5

Research in the Humanities

Resources in the Humanities

INDEXES AND DATABASES FOR THE HUMANITIES

Arts and Humanities Citation Index. 1976–. Indexes citations in articles from over a thousand periodicals in the humanities and arts; entries allow tracing influence through later citations of books and periodicals. (online by subscription, CD-ROM)

Essay and General Literature Index. 1900–. Indexes authors and subjects of separate essays published in collections. (Essays are not usually listed separately in library catalogs.) (online by subscription, CD-ROM)

Humanities Index. 1974–. Formerly *Social Sciences and Humanities Index,* 1965–74, and *International Index,* 1907–65. Indexes and abstracts (only on CD-ROM) articles and book reviews from about three hundred periodicals covering literature, history, the arts, the classics, and other topics in the humanities. (online by subscription, CD-ROM)

WEB RESOURCES FOR THE HUMANITIES

EDSITEment
<http://edsitement.neh.fed.us>
Links to twenty high-quality humanities Web sites, selected under the auspices of the National Endowment for the Humanities.

Infomine: Scholarly Internet Resource Collections
    <http://infomine.ucr.edu>
    Supplies indexed and annotated links to databases and other resources of academic interest in the humanities, performing arts, and visual arts.

Voice of the Shuttle: Web Page for Humanities Research
    <http://vos.ucsb.edu>
    Includes highlights, top sites, and links to extensive resources for general or specialized research in the humanities.

The Webliography: Internet Subject Guides
    <http://www.lib.lsu.edu/weblio.html#Humanities>
    Provides extensive annotated guides to Web resources in many fields in the humanities, including art, film, theater, literature, history, music, classics, and others.

Art and Architecture

GENERAL REFERENCE SOURCES FOR ART AND ARCHITECTURE

Encyclopedia of Architecture: Design, Engineering, and Construction. 5 vols. 1988–90. Supplies articles, including bibliographies, on architectural history, technology, construction, and design.

Encyclopedia of Artists. 6 vols. 2000. Provides an illustrated introduction to Western art, with entries on artists, works, and major periods from the Middle Ages through the present.

Encyclopedia of World Art. 15 vols. plus supplements. 1959–68; 1983; 1987. Includes articles, many illustrated, on artists, art history, art in other cultures and societies, and related topics.

The Grove Dictionary of Art. 34 vols. 2002. Examines all the visual arts except film, with 15,000 illustrations.

McGraw-Hill Dictionary of Art. 1969. Supplies definitions and longer articles, including illustrations.

Oxford Dictionary of Art. 1997. Provides entries on the Western fine and decorative arts, including artists, terms, and institutions.

INDEXES AND DATABASES FOR ART AND ARCHITECTURE

ARTBibliographies Modern. 1974–. Lists and abstracts articles, books, and catalogs about art. (online by subscription)

Art Index. 1929–. Indexes articles from about 250 periodicals on the fine arts, archaeology, architecture, interior design, city planning, photography, film, and other topics. (online by subscription, CD-ROM)

Art Information: Research Methods and Resources. 1990. Lists major and specialized resources, both printed and electronic, and explains how to use them.

Avery Index to Architectural Periodicals. 1965–. Contains citations to articles in architecture and design, archaeology, city planning, interior design, and historic preservation. (online by subscription, CD-ROM)

BHA: Bibliography of the History of Art. 1991–. Formerly *RILA (Répertoire internationale de la littérature de l'art),* 1975–89, and *RAA (Répertoire d'art et d'archéologie),* 1910–63. Lists articles from about four thousand periodicals plus books, papers, and other materials about the arts. (online by subscription as *Art Literature International*)

Fine Arts: A Bibliographic Guide to Basic Reference Books. 1990. Lists and annotates references to resources in the fine arts.

GROVEart. An online subscription service that provides access to a quarterly updated online version of *The Dictionary of Art* (34 vols., 2000) and includes articles on artists, movements, and works in the fine and decorative arts worldwide, as well as image links and a search engine.

WEB RESOURCES FOR ART AND ARCHITECTURE

Architecture and Building
<http://library.nevada.edu/arch/rsrce/webrsrce/contents.html>
Organizes extensive topical and alphabetical listings of Web resources on architecture and related issues.

The Art History Research Centre
<http://www-fofa.concordia.ca/arth/AHRC/index.htm>
Introduces Internet research in art history and links to many resources such as Internet art collections, library catalogs, periodical indexes, newsgroups, and other art history servers.

Art History Resources on the Web
> <http://witcombe.sbc.edu/ARTHLinks.html>
> Provides an extraordinarily detailed set of chronologically organized links to art history sources, from prehistoric through modern.

Art Museum Network
> <http://www.amn.org>
> Free access to information about collections, exhibitions, and services of the world's largest and most prestigious art museums.

The Getty Information Institute
> <http://www.getty.edu/research>
> Provides access to major databases and indexes on art and cultural history, including specialized search tools and numerous graphic images with reference pages.

H-Gig Art History
> <http://www.ucr.edu/h-gig/hist-art/arthi.html>
> Supplies easy links to some of the best art history sources and directories, based in the large HORUS system at the University of California at Riverside; smaller and more manageable than some of the full-service sites.

History of Art Virtual Library
> <http://www.chart.ac.uk/vlib>
> Includes links to art history sites, museums, galleries, art history organizations, and university art departments.

National Gallery of Art
> <http://www.nga.gov/>
> Supplies images from the collection and news about current displays and educational opportunities.

Virtual Library Museums Pages
> <http://vlmp.museophile.com>
> Includes a large number of links to recent and current exhibitions at many major museums, by country.

World Art Treasures
> <http://www.bergerfoundation.ch/>
> Offers in-depth links to selected artists' works and areas of art, with good links to other sites.

World Wide Arts Resources
<http://world-arts-resources.com/>
Contains extensive links and search capability to artists, art history, museums, and other art-related topics.

The WWW Virtual Library—Architecture
<http://www.clr.toronto.ca/VIRTALLIB/arch.html>
Supplies links to varied resources on architecture, landscape architecture, architectural engineering, and related topics.

WWW Virtual Library—Art
<http://www.icom.org/vlmp/galleries.html>
Provides an excellent collection of links to both art and literature sites, including links to other virtual libraries.

Classics

GENERAL REFERENCE SOURCES FOR THE CLASSICS

Oxford Classical Dictionary. 1996. Supplies articles with bibliographies on classical figures, literature, places, and events.

Oxford Companion to Classical Civilization. 1998. Includes articles on classical writers, major works and characters, literary forms, and mythology, as well as background information on classical history, geography, religion, politics, and social context.

INDEXES AND DATABASES FOR THE CLASSICS

L'Année Philologique. 1928–. Indexes periodical articles, books, and other resources about classical language, literature, history, law, science, culture, and other topics. (CD-ROM)

WEB RESOURCES FOR THE CLASSICS

Ancient World Web
<http://www.julen.net/ancient/>
Includes an extensive list of linked sites on the ancient world and its modern connections, indexed by geographical and subject areas.

Argos: Limited Area Search of the Ancient and Medieval Internet
<http://argos.evansville.edu>
Provides a limited-area search engine to peer-reviewed sites on the ancient and medieval worlds.

Classics and Mediterranean Archaeology
<http://rome.classics.lsa.umich.edu/welcome.html>
Provides links to widely varied resources on texts, field sites, projects, images, archaeological excavations, exhibitions, museums, academic institutions, maps, publications, and other information on classical studies.

Classics at Oxford
<http://www.classics.ox.ac.uk/resources.html>
Provides links to many resources in the classics and ancient history; has search capability.

Internet Resources for Classical Studies and Classical Languages
<http://www.brynmawr.edu/Library/Docs/classics.html>
Contains links (with search capability) to online texts and journals and other resources related to the classics.

The Perseus Project
<http://www.perseus.tufts.edu>
Supplies extensive information on the ancient world, including background information, Greek texts and translations, maps, descriptions, and over thirteen thousand images of vases, coins, buildings, sculptures, and site plans.

History

GENERAL REFERENCE SOURCES FOR HISTORY

Cambridge Ancient History. 12 vols. 1939–82, with later revisions. Includes articles, illustrations, maps, and other supporting materials in volumes on early civilization in Europe and the Middle East; additional volumes supply illustrations and appendices.

Cambridge Encyclopedia of Latin America and the Caribbean. 1992. Supplies articles on the history, politics, economics, and culture of the region.

Cambridge History of Africa. 8 vols. 1975–86. Covers African history chronologically from early times through the mid-1970s.

Cambridge Medieval History. 9 vols. 1911–75. Covers the major events and changes in medieval history, including government, religion, and cultural background.

Chambers Dictionary of World History. 2001. Contains over 7,500 entries on key figures and events of world history, with an in-depth focus on the period between A.D. 1000 and 2000; includes maps, tables, and family trees.

Dictionary of Concepts in History. 1986. Supplies articles on major historical concepts, including definitions, histories of the concepts, and additional sources of information.

Dictionary of the Middle Ages. 13 vols. 1982–89. Provides authoritative articles with bibliographies on many people and topics relating to the culture, politics, and religion of the medieval period (A.D. 500–1500).

Encyclopedia of American Social History. 3 vols. 1993. Includes articles and bibliographies on aspects of ordinary life, work, and leisure.

Encyclopedia of Asian History. 4 vols. 1988. Supplies articles, often with bibliographies for further research in English, including major figures and wide-ranging topics about Asian history and civilization from early times on.

Encyclopedia of the Renaissance. 1987. Offers brief entries on the Renaissance, including historical, political, and other topics.

Encyclopedia of World History. 1999. Contains entries on events, figures, and concepts from prehistoric through modern times; includes cross-references, maps, portraits, and engravings.

The Oxford Companion to British History. 1997. Provides entries on social, political, cultural, economic, and scientific events, both national and local and from 55 B.C. to the 1990s; includes maps and genealogical charts.

The Oxford Companion to United States History. 2001. Examines major figures, events, ideologies, and developments in technology, the economy, immigration, and urbanization from before 1492 to the end of the twentieth century.

The Oxford Dictionary of World History. 2000. Covers key figures, subjects, and events from prehistoric to modern times in concise entries; includes detailed maps on particular events and topics.

United States History: A Selective Guide to Information Sources. 1994. Offers a topically arranged annotated list of the reference works published in the previous two hundred years on the subject of U.S. history, including print sources, online databases, and CD-ROMs.

INDEXES AND DATABASES FOR HISTORY

America: History and Life. 1964–. Formerly in *History Abstracts,* 1954–63. Indexes and abstracts articles from more than two thousand periodicals on the history and culture of North America (United States and Canada), including local, regional, and national coverage. (online by subscription, CD-ROM)

Handbook for Research in American History: A Guide to Bibliographies and Other Reference Books. 1994. Lists reference sources covering many aspects of American history.

Harvard Guide to American History. 2 vols. 1974. Supplies research guidance and lists major sources about notable people and topics as diverse as social context, religion, and law; volume 2 chronologically surveys U.S. history.

Historical Abstracts. 1955–. Indexes and abstracts articles from more than two thousand periodicals and books on history, culture, historical research methods, and regional, national, and worldwide topics from 1450 on, excluding North America. (online by subscription, CD-ROM)

Reference Sources in History: An Introductory Guide. 1990. Lists and annotates resources for studying history worldwide in all periods.

WEB RESOURCES FOR HISTORY

Eurodocs
<http://library.byu.edu/~rdh/eurodocs/homepage.html>
Offers primary historical documents from western Europe; organized by country.

Gateway to World History
<http://www.history.ccsu.edu/History_web_links.htm>
Supports searches for teachers and students of world history, and allows links to more specific areas.

Gopher Jewels History Menu
   <gopher://cwis.usc.edu/11/other_gophers_and_information
   _resources/gophers_by_subject/gopher_jewels/academic/history>
   Allows downloading of original archival documents from a variety of
   U.S. and world history sources.

Historical Text Archive
   <http://historicaltextarchive.com/>
   Provides access to many world history texts; organized by both area
   and topic.

History @ Bedford/St. Martin's
   <http://www.bedford/stmartins.com/history>
   Provides an annotated list of links to history sites.

The History Net
   <http://www.theHistoryNet.com/>
   A project of the National Historical Society. Provides a historical
   magazine as well as a search service.

Internet History Sourcebooks Project
   <http://www.fordham.edu/hasall/>
   Collections of public domain and copy-permitted historical texts for
   educational use.

The Library of Congress: American Memory
   <http://memory.loc.gov/ammem/amhome.html>
   An extensive site with text and links to millions of primary-source
   items (including maps, photos, and documents) from the Library of
   Congress and other collections; has excellent search capabilities.

World History Archives
   <http://www.hartford-hwp.com/archives/>
   Offers access to actual versions of important texts in world history
   and many links to contemporary writings.

The WWW Virtual Library—History
   <http://www.ku.edu/history/VL/>
   Provides links to history servers by subject research, eras and
   epochs, historical topics, and countries and regions; includes search
   capability.

Literature

GENERAL REFERENCE SOURCES FOR LITERATURE

The Cambridge History of American Literature. 1994–. Covers poetry, prose, and literary criticism from 1590 to the present in multiple volumes that include thematically arranged entries on works of writers, critics, and scholars.

Dictionary of Literary Biography. 1978–. Supplies articles, including bibliographies and photographs, on the major writers representing each period or topic covered.

Encyclopedia of Folklore and Literature. 1998. Includes entries about authors, works, scholars, and movements of folklore and literature throughout the world.

The Encyclopedia of the Novel. 2 vols. 1998. Focuses on the development of the novel througout the world and includes over 600 essays on writers and novels, as well as regional histories of the novel. (online by subscription to Chadwyck-Healy LION database)

Harper Handbook of Literature. 1997. Provides a dictionary of literary terms, concepts, genres, and movements with a mixture of brief entries and longer entries with bibliographies.

Oxford Companion to American Literature. 1995. Supplies articles on authors, works, characters, and other literary topics, as well as on related background topics.

Oxford Companion to English Literature. 2000. Supplies articles on literary topics, terms, authors, works, characters, movements, trends, and influences.

Readers Guide to Literature in English. 2000. Includes entries on writers, literary devices, genres, movements, criticism, and the literatures of various groups, regions, and time periods.

INDEXES AND DATABASES FOR LITERATURE

MLA International Bibliography of Books and Articles on the Modern Languages and Literature. 1921–. Indexes articles from over three thousand periodicals plus books and dissertations on literature and language, including literary works, authors, national literatures, literary movements and themes, literary theory and criticism, linguistics, and related topics. (online by subscription, CD-ROM)

Reference Works in British and American Literature. 2 vols. 1990–91. Lists and annotates publications and other resources for studying literary topics and specific authors.

WEB RESOURCES FOR LITERATURE

American Studies Web
<http://www.georgetown.edu/crossroads/asw/lit.html>
Provides links to many elements of American studies, with an emphasis on literary texts, authors, approaches, genres, and associations.

In Other Words: A Lexicon of the Humanities
<http://www.sil.org/humanities/>
Provides an interesting hyperlinked lexicon and glossary of major terms in literary criticism, rhetoric, and linguistics.

International Gay and Lesbian Review
<http://www.usc.edu/isd/archives/oneigla/onepress>
Provides abstracts and reviews of many books related to lesbian, gay, bisexual, and transgender studies.

Literary Resources on the Net
<http://newark.rutgers.edu/~jlynch/Lit/>
Allows you to search for literary materials on the Net and provides a list of periodicals and genre-based categories to explore.

Project Gutenberg Master Index
<http://promo.net/pg/>
Offers the best current index to PG texts, most of which are now in the public domain.

Resources for Russian and Slavic Languages and Literature
<http://www.library.vanderbilt.edu/central/russian.html#russian>
Provides links to Web sites, dictionaries, literary sites, e-journals, e-texts, departments, and professional organizations.

Romance Languages Resources Page
> <http://humanities.uchicago.edu/depts/romance/resources/resources.html>
> Offers links to cultural and textual resources and to sites that help those studying Romance languages.

Music

GENERAL REFERENCE SOURCES FOR MUSIC

New Grove Dictionary of Music and Musicians. 20 vols. 2001. Supplies entries on thousands of musicians and music topics, including bibliographies, lists of works, maps, family trees, and illustrations of instruments. (online by subscription)

New Oxford Companion to Music. 2 vols. 1983. Provides entries defining musical terms, types of music, aspects of music history, and related topics.

New Oxford History of Music. 9 vols. 1986–90. Covers music, ancient through modern, including bibliographies and music examples.

INDEXES AND DATABASES FOR MUSIC

Music: A Guide to the Reference Literature. 1987. Supplies annotated lists of reference sources about music, including bibliographies, discographies, periodicals, and music organizations.

Music Index: A Subject-Author Guide to Current Music Periodical Literature. 1949–. Indexes articles from over three hundred periodicals on music and musicians. (CD-ROM)

Music Reference and Research Materials: An Annotated Bibliography. 1993. Lists standard reference sources about music.

RILM Abstracts of Music Literature. 1966–. Indexes and abstracts articles, books, and other sources. (online by subscription, CD-ROM as *Muse*)

WEB RESOURCES FOR MUSIC

Classical Music on the Web
> <http://classicalusa.com>
> Offers an "organized jumpstation" to the best classical music sites on the Web.

Internet Resources for Music Scholars
<http://hcl.harvard.edu/loebmusic/online-in-intro.html>
Contains links, with search capability, to databases, journals, and many other music-related sites.

Sibelius Academy Music Resources
<http://www.siba.fi/Kulttuuripalvelut/music.html>
Provides links to every aspect of music appreciation, production, and education.

Worldwide Internet Music Resources
<http://www.music.indiana.edu/music_resources/>
Includes a general list of links to musicians, composers, performance sites, genres, research, industry, and journals.

Philosophy and Religion

GENERAL REFERENCE SOURCES FOR PHILOSOPHY AND RELIGION

The Cambridge Dictionary of Philosophy. 1999. Surveys key concepts and figures in both Western and non-Western philosophy, with extensive coverage of contemporary philosophers and new fields of thought.

Dictionary of Philosophy. 1984. Supplies entries on key terms and notable philosophers.

Encyclopedia of Philosophy. 4 vols. 1973. Includes articles and bibliographies on philosophers and topics of significance in the field.

Encyclopedia of Religion. 16 vols. 1987. Provides articles and bibliographies on both historical and present-day religions worldwide, including beliefs, practices, and major figures and groups.

The Routledge Encyclopedia of Philosophy. 10 vols. 1998. Contains entries on concepts, scholarship, schools, and themes of world philosophy and religion. (online by subscription)

INDEXES AND DATABASES FOR PHILOSOPHY AND RELIGION

Philosopher's Index. 1967–. Indexes and abstracts books and articles from about three hundred periodicals. (online by subscription, CD-ROM)

Philosophy: A Guide to the Reference Literature. 1986. Supplies annotated entries on reference works in philosophy.

Religion Index. 1975–. Formerly *Index to Religious Periodical Literature,* 1949–76. Indexes and abstracts books and articles from several hundred periodicals. (online by subscription, CD-ROM)

Religious and Theological Abstracts. 1958–. Indexes and abstracts articles from several hundred periodicals. (CD-ROM)

Religious Information Sources: A Worldwide Guide. 1992. Lists sources for all world religions.

WEB RESOURCES FOR PHILOSOPHY AND RELIGION

American Philosophical Association Home Page
    <http://www.udel.edu/apa>
    Includes Web resources with guides to philosophy, philosophers, texts, journals, and academic organizations.

Guide to Philosophy on the Internet
    <http://www.earlham.edu/~peters/philinks.htm>
    Includes links to sites with philosophy guides (in various languages), philosophers, journals, organizations, dictionaries, and many topics dealing with philosophy.

Hippias: Limited Area Search of Philosophy on the Internet
    <http://hippias.evansville.edu>
    Provides keyword searches as well as links to associated sites and search tools.

Philosophy in Cyberspace
    <http://www-personal.monash.edu.au/~dey/phil>
    Indexes, organizes, and annotates resources on philosophy topics, electronic and print journals, encyclopedias, organizations, and many other linked materials; includes search capability.

Religion and Philosophy Resources on the Internet
    <http://www.bu.edu/sth/library/resources.html>
    Offers selected annotated links to resources on philosophy and religion, including Christianity, Judaism, Islam, and Asian religions.

Religion (Humanities): Galaxy
    <http://www.galaxy.com/cgi-bin/dirlist?node=27725>
    Supplies access to collections of resources and directories for the study of religion.

The WWW Virtual Library—Philosophy
    <http://www.bris.ac.uk/Depts/Philosophy/VL/>
    Provides links to thousands of sources, including articles, journals, books, databases, and discussion groups; allows searches.

Theater and Film

GENERAL REFERENCE SOURCES FOR THEATER AND FILM

The Concise Oxford Companion to the Theatre. 1992. Supplies essays on theater history and style, buildings, dramatists, performers, directors, festivals, and technology.

Film Encyclopedia. 1994. Supplies biographical and topical entries on many aspects of film.

McGraw-Hill Encyclopedia of World Drama. 5 vols. 1984. Supplies extensive articles, including bibliographies, on playwrights, theaters, genres, dramatic terms, regional drama, and related topics.

INDEXES AND DATABASES FOR THEATER AND FILM

Film Literature Index. 1973–. Indexes articles from several hundred periodicals on film, television, and video.

International Index to Film Periodicals. 1972–. Indexes articles, interviews, and reviews from more than eighty-five periodicals, with entries divided into three sections: general subjects, individual films, and biography. (online by subscription)

WEB RESOURCES FOR THEATER AND FILM

McCoy's Brief Guide to Internet Resources in Theatre and Performance Studies
    <http://www.stetson.edu/departments/csata/thr_guid.html>
    Supplies useful research resources on topics such as acting, stagecraft, playwrights, and plays, as well as an annotated list of especially helpful sites.

Playbill On-line
<http://www.playbill.com>
Covers theater news, awards, and listings, and provides links through Theatre Central to a directory of resources on playwrights, stagecraft, Shakespeare, theater companies, casting calls, publications, and other varied topics.

Theatre Resources at ELAC (East Los Angeles College)
<http://www.perspicacity.com/elactheatre/elacpage.htm>
Includes a wide range of resources on plays, playwrights, characters, costumes, acting, directing, and other topics, with links to other sites.

World Wide Arts Resources: Theater
<http://wwar.com/categories/Theater>
Provides numerous links, by category, to most aspects of theater, including acting, choreography, plays, Broadway theater, and opera; has search capability.

The WWW Virtual Library: Theatre and Drama
<http://vl-theatre/com>
Provides international theater resources (including studies, collections of images, events, companies, and academic institutions) and also indexes plays available online.

MLA Style

This section discusses the Modern Language Association (MLA) style of documentation, widely used in literature and languages as well as other fields.

For more information on MLA style, consult the MLA's Web site, <www.mla.org>, or one of the following books.

Gibaldi, Joseph. *MLA Handbook for Writers of Research Papers.* 6th ed. New York: MLA, 2003.

Gibaldi, Joseph. *MLA Style Manual and Guide to Scholarly Publishing.* 2nd ed. New York: MLA, 1998.

MLA Format for In-Text Citations

MLA style requires documentation in the text of an essay for every quotation, paraphrase, summary, or other material that must be cited. In-text citations document material from other sources with both *signal phrases* and *parenthetical references.* Signal phrases introduce the material, often including the author's name. Parenthetical references direct you to full bibliographic entries in a list of works cited at the end of the text. *(Text continues on page 79.)*

DIRECTORY TO MLA STYLE

In-Text Citations

1. Author named in a signal phrase, 79
2. Author named in a parenthetical reference, 79
3. Two or three authors, 79
4. Four or more authors, 80
5. Corporate or group author, 80
6. Unknown author, 80
7. Author of two or more works, 81
8. Two or more authors with the same surname, 81
9. Multivolume work, 81
10. Literary work, 82
11. Work in an anthology, 82
12. Sacred text, 83
13. Indirect source, 83
14. Two or more sources in the same reference, 83
15. Entire work or one-page article, 84
16. Work without page numbers, 84
17. Electronic or nonprint source, 84

Explanatory and Bibliographic Notes

(Continued)

List of Works Cited

BOOKS

1. One author, 87
2. Two or three authors, 87
3. Four or more authors, 88
4. Corporate or group author, 88
5. Unknown author, 88
6. Two or more books by the same author(s), 88
7. Editor or editors, 89
8. Author and editor, 89
9. Work in an anthology or chapter in a book with an editor, 90
10. Two or more items from an anthology, 90
11. Translation, 91
12. Edition other than the first, 91
13. One volume of a multivolume work, 92
14. Two or more volumes of a multivolume work, 92
15. Preface, foreword, introduction, or afterword, 92
16. Entry in a reference work, 92
17. Book that is part of a series, 93
18. Republication, 93
19. Government document, 93
20. Pamphlet, 94
21. Published proceedings of a conference, 94
22. Publisher's imprint, 95
23. Title within the title, 95
24. Sacred text, 95

PERIODICALS

25. Article in a journal paginated by volume, 96
26. Article in a journal paginated by issue, 97
27. Article in a monthly magazine, 97
28. Article in a weekly magazine, 97
29. Article in a newspaper, 97
30. Editorial or letter to the editor, 98
31. Unsigned article, 98
32. Two or more articles by the same author(s), 98
33. Review, 99
34. Article with a title within the title, 99

(Continued)

ELECTRONIC SOURCES
35. Document from a Web site, *101*
36. Entire Web site, *101*
37. Course, department, or personal site, *102*
38. Online book, *102*
39. Online government document, *103*
40. Article in an online periodical, *104*
41. Work from an online subscription service, *104*
42. Posting to a discussion group, *106*
43. Email, *106*
44. Synchronous communication, *106*
45. Other electronic sources, *107*
46. Periodically revised database on CD-ROM, *107*
47. Single-issue CD-ROM, diskette, or magnetic tape, *108*
48. Multidisc CD-ROM, *108*
49. Work in an indeterminate medium, *108*
50. Software or computer program, *109*

OTHER KINDS OF SOURCES
51. Unpublished dissertation or thesis, *109*
52. Published dissertation, *109*
53. Article from a microform, *110*
54. Interview, *110*
55. Letter, *110*
56. Film, video, or DVD, *111*
57. Television or radio program, *111*
58. Sound recording, *112*
59. Work of art or photograph, *112*
60. Lecture or speech, *113*
61. Performance, *113*
62. Map or chart, *113*
63. Cartoon or comic strip, *114*
64. Advertisement, *114*

A Student Research Essay, MLA Style

In general, make parenthetical references short, including just enough information for your readers to locate the full reference in the works-cited list. Place a parenthetical reference as near the relevant material as possible without disrupting the flow of the sentence. Note in the following examples *where* punctuation is placed in relation to the parentheses. Except for block quotations, place any punctuation mark *after* the closing parenthesis. If you are referring to a quotation, place the parenthetical reference *after* the closing quotation mark but *before* any other punctuation mark. For block quotations, place the reference one space after the final punctuation mark. Here are examples of the ways to cite various kinds of sources:

1. AUTHOR NAMED IN A SIGNAL PHRASE

Ordinarily, use the author's name in a signal phrase to introduce the material, and simply cite the page number(s) in parentheses. Use the full name the first time you cite a source. For later references, use just the last name.

```
Herrera indicates that Kahlo believed in a
"vitalistic form of pantheism" (328).
```

2. AUTHOR NAMED IN A PARENTHETICAL REFERENCE

When you do not name the author in the text, include the author's last name before the page number(s) in the parentheses.

```
In places, Beauvoir "sees Marxists as believing
in subjectivity as much as existentialists do"
(Whitmarsh 63).
```

3. TWO OR THREE AUTHORS

Use all the last names in a signal phrase or parenthetical reference.

> Gortner, Hebrun, and Nicolson maintain that
> "opinion leaders" influence other people in an
> organization because they are respected, not
> because they hold high positions (175).

4. FOUR OR MORE AUTHORS

Use the first author's name and *et al.* ("and others") in a signal phrase or parenthetical reference or, preferably, name all the authors.

> Similarly, as Belenky, Clinchy, Goldberger, and
> Tarule assert, examining the lives of women
> expands our understanding of human development
> (7).

5. CORPORATE OR GROUP AUTHOR

Give the corporation's name or a shortened form in a signal phrase or parenthetical reference.

> In fact, one of the leading foundations in the
> field of higher education supports the recent
> proposals for community-run public schools
> (Carnegie Corporation 45).

6. UNKNOWN AUTHOR

Use the title of the work or a shortened version in a signal phrase or parenthetical reference.

> "Hype," by one analysis, is "an artificially
> engendered atmosphere of hysteria" ("Today's
> Marketplace" 51).

7. AUTHOR OF TWO OR MORE WORKS

If your list of works cited has more than one work by the same author, give the title of the work you are citing or a shortened version in a signal phrase or parenthetical reference.

```
Gardner presents readers with their own silliness
through his description of a "pointless,
ridiculous monster, crouched in the shadows,
stinking of dead men, murdered children, and
martyred cows" (Grendel 2).
```

8. TWO OR MORE AUTHORS WITH THE SAME SURNAME

If your list of works cited includes works by authors with the same surname, always include each author's first name in the signal phrases or parenthetical references for those works.

```
Children will learn to write if they are allowed
to choose their own subjects, James Britton
asserts, citing the Schools Council study of the
1960s (37-42).
```

9. MULTIVOLUME WORK

In the parenthetical reference, note the volume number first and then page number(s), with a colon and one space between them.

```
Modernist writers prized experimentation and
gradually even sought to blur the line between
poetry and prose, according to Forster
(3: 150).
```

If you name only one volume of the work in your list of works cited, you need include only the page number in the parentheses.

10. LITERARY WORK

Because literary works are often available in many different editions, first cite the page number(s) from the edition you used followed by a semicolon, and then give other identifying information that will lead readers to the passage in any edition. Indicate the act and/or scene in a play (*37; sc. 1*). For a novel, indicate the part or chapter (*175; ch. 4*).

```
In utter despair, Dostoyevsky's character Mitya
wonders aloud about the "terrible tragedies
realism inflicts on people" (376; bk. 8, ch. 2).
```

For a poem, instead of page numbers cite the part (if there is one) and line(s), separated by a period. If you are citing only line numbers, use the word *line(s)* in the first citation of the poem (*lines 33–34*).

```
On dying, Whitman speculates "All goes onward and
outward, nothing collapses, / And to die is
different from what any one supposed, and
luckier" (6.129-30).
```

For a verse play, give only the act, scene, and line numbers, separated by periods.

```
As Macbeth begins, the witches greet Banquo as
"Lesser than Macbeth, and greater" (1.3.65).
```

11. WORK IN AN ANTHOLOGY

For an essay, short story, or other piece of prose reprinted in an anthology, use the name of the author of the work, not the editor of the anthology, but use the page number(s) from the anthology.

```
Narratives of captivity play a major role in
early writing by women in the United States, as
demonstrated by Silko (219).
```

12. SACRED TEXT

To cite a sacred text such as the Qur'an or the Bible, give the title of the edition you used, the book, and the chapter and verse (or their equivalent) separated by a period. In your text, spell out the names of books. In a parenthetical reference, use an abbreviation for books with names of five or more letters (*Gen.* for *Genesis*).

```
He ignored the admonition "Pride goes before
destruction, and a haughty spirit before a fall"
(New Oxford Annotated Bible, Prov. 16.18).
```

13. INDIRECT SOURCE

Use the abbreviation *qtd. in* to indicate that you are quoting from someone else's report of a conversation, interview, letter, or the like.

```
As Arthur Miller says, "When somebody is
destroyed everybody finally contributes to it,
but in Willy's case, the end product would be
virtually the same" (qtd. in Martin and Meyer
375).
```

14. TWO OR MORE SOURCES IN THE SAME REFERENCE

Separate the information with semicolons.

```
Some economists recommend that employment be
redefined to include unpaid domestic labor (Clark
148; Nevins 39).
```

15. ENTIRE WORK OR ONE-PAGE ARTICLE

Include the reference in the text without any page numbers or parentheses.

```
Michael Ondaatje's poetic sensibility transfers
beautifully to prose in The English Patient.
```

16. WORK WITHOUT PAGE NUMBERS

If a work has no page numbers but has another kind of numbered sections, include in parentheses the name and number(s) of any specific one(s) you are citing, such as paragraph parts (*pt.* or *pts.*), or screens. If such a reference includes the author's name, use a comma after the name.

```
Whitman considered their speech "a source of a
native grand opera," in the words of Ellison
(par. 13).
```

17. ELECTRONIC OR NONPRINT SOURCE

Give enough information in a signal phrase or parenthetical reference for readers to locate the source in the list of works cited. Usually use the name or title under which you list the source. If you are citing any specific section(s), include the page, part, paragraph, or screen number(s) in parentheses.

```
Describing children's language acquisition,
Pinker explains that "what's innate about
language is just a way of paying attention to
parental speech" (Johnson, sec. 1).
```

MLA Format for Explanatory and Bibliographic Notes

MLA style allows explanatory notes for information or commentary that would not readily fit into the text but is needed for clarification or further explanation. In addition, MLA style permits bibliographic notes for citing several sources for one point and for offering thanks to, information about, or evaluation of a source. Superscript numbers are used in the text to refer readers to the notes, which may appear as endnotes (typed under the heading "Notes" on a separate page after the text but before the list of works cited) or as footnotes at the bottom of the page (typed four lines below the last text line). For example:

SUPERSCRIPT NUMBER IN TEXT

```
Stewart emphasizes the existence of social
contacts in Hawthorne's life so that the audience
will accept a different Hawthorne, one more
attuned to modern times than the figure in
Woodberry.[3]
```

NOTE

```
    [3] Woodberry does, however, show that
Hawthorne was often an unsociable individual. He
emphasizes the seclusion of Hawthorne's mother,
who separated herself from her family after the
death of her husband, often even taking meals
alone (28). Woodberry seems to imply that Mrs.
Hawthorne's isolation rubbed off onto her son.
```

MLA Format for a List of Works Cited

Works Cited is an alphabetical list of the sources cited in your essay. (If your instructor asks that you list everything you have read as background, call the list *Works Consulted*.) Here are some guidelines for preparing such a list:

- Start your list on a separate page after the text of your essay and any notes.
- Number each page, continuing the page numbers of the text.
- Center the heading *Works Cited* an inch from the top of the page; do not underline or italicize it or enclose it in quotation marks. Double-space between the heading and the first entry, and double-space the entire list.
- Start each entry flush with the left margin, and indent any additional lines one-half inch, or five spaces.
- List your sources alphabetically by author's (or editor's) last name. If the author of a source is unknown, alphabetize the source by the first word of the title, disregarding *A, An,* or *The.*

If you are using software (Microsoft Word, EndNote, Research Assistant) to record and create a list of works cited, double-check that all formatting is accurate.

The sample works-cited entries that follow observe MLA's advice to underline words that are often italicized in print. Although most computers can generate italics easily, the MLA recommends that "you can avoid ambiguity by using underlining" in your research essays where the "type style of every letter and punctuation mark must be easily recognizable." If you wish to use italics instead, first check with your instructor.

Books

The basic entry for a book includes three elements, each followed by a period.

- *Author.* List the last name first, followed by a comma and the first name.
- *Title.* Underline or (if your instructor permits) italicize the title and any subtitle, and capitalize all major words.
- *Publication information.* Give the city of publication followed by a colon, a space, and a shortened version of the publisher's name—dropping *Books, Press, Publishers, Inc.,* and so on (*Harper* for *HarperCollins Publishers*); using only the first surname (*Harcourt* for *Harcourt Brace*); and abbreviating *University Press* (*Oxford UP* for *Oxford University Press*). The publisher's name is followed by a comma and the year of publication.

Here is an example of a basic entry for a book:

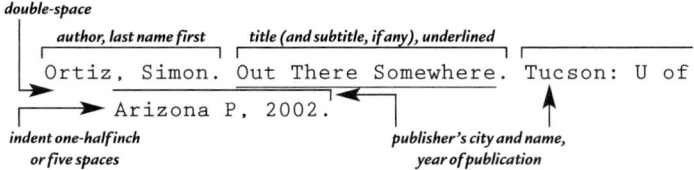

1. ONE AUTHOR

deCordova, Richard. <u>Picture Personalities: The Emergence of the Star System in America.</u> Urbana: U of Illinois P, 1990.

2. TWO OR THREE AUTHORS

List the first author, last name first; then list the name(s) of the other author(s) in regular order, with a comma between authors and an *and* before the last one.

```
Appleby, Joyce, Lynn Hunt, and Margaret Jacob.
     Telling the Truth about History. New York:
     Norton, 1994.
```

3. FOUR OR MORE AUTHORS

Give the first author listed on the title page, followed by a comma and *et al.* ("and others"), or list all the names, since the use of *et al.* diminishes the importance of the other contributors.

```
Belenky, Mary Field, Blythe Clinchy, Jill
     Goldberger, and Nancy Tarule. Women's Ways
     of Knowing. New York: Basic, 1986.
```

4. CORPORATE OR GROUP AUTHOR

Give the name of the group listed on the title page as the author, even if the same group published the book.

```
American Chemical Society. Handbook for Authors
     of Papers in the American Chemical Society
     Publications. Washington: Amer. Chemical
     Soc., 1978.
```

5. UNKNOWN AUTHOR

Begin the entry with the title.

```
The New York Times Atlas of the World. New York:
     New York Times, 1980.
```

6. TWO OR MORE BOOKS BY THE SAME AUTHOR(S)

Arrange the entries alphabetically by title. Include the name(s) of the author(s) in the first entry, but in subsequent entries use three hyphens followed by a period.

```
Lorde, Audre. A Burst of Light. Ithaca:
     Firebrand, 1988.
---. Sister Outsider. Trumansburg: Crossing,
     1984.
```

If you cite a work by one author who is also listed as the first coauthor of another work you cite, list the single-author work first, and repeat the author's name in the entry for the coauthored work. Also repeat the author's name if you cite a work in which that author is listed as the first of a different set of coauthors. Use three hyphens only when the work is by *exactly* the same author(s) as the previous entry.

7. EDITOR OR EDITORS

Treat an editor as an author, but add a comma and *ed.* (or *eds.* for more than one editor).

```
Wall, Cheryl A., ed. Changing Our Own Words:
     Essays on Criticism, Theory, and Writing by
     Black Women. New Brunswick: Rutgers UP,
     1989.
```

8. AUTHOR AND EDITOR

If you have cited the body of the text, begin with the author's name, and list the editor's name, introduced by *Ed.,* after the title.

```
James, Henry. Portrait of a Lady. Ed. Leon Edel.
     Boston: Houghton, 1963.
```

If you have cited the editor's contribution to the work, begin with the editor's name followed by a comma and *ed.,* and list the author's name, introduced by *By,* after the title.

```
Edel, Leon, ed. Portrait of a Lady. By Henry
    James. Boston: Houghton, 1963.
```

9. WORK IN AN ANTHOLOGY OR CHAPTER IN A BOOK WITH AN EDITOR

List the author(s) of the selection or chapter; its title; the title of the book in which the selection or chapter appears; *Ed.* and the name(s) of the editor(s); the publication information; and the inclusive page numbers of the selection or chapter.

```
Gordon, Mary. "The Parable of the Cave." The
    Writer on Her Work. Ed. Janet Sternburg. New
    York: Norton, 1980. 27-32.
```

If the selection was originally published in a periodical and you are asked to supply information for this original source, use the following format. *Rpt.* is the abbreviation for "Reprinted."

```
Didion, Joan. "Why I Write." New York Times Book
    Review 9 Dec. 1976: 22. Rpt. in The Writer
    on Her Work. Ed. Janet Sternburg. New York:
    Norton, 1980. 3-16.
```

For inclusive page numbers up to 99, note all digits in the second number. For numbers above 99, note only the last two digits and any others that change in the second number (*115–18, 1378–79, 296–301*).

10. TWO OR MORE ITEMS FROM AN ANTHOLOGY

Include the anthology itself in your list of works cited.

```
Donalson, Melvin, ed. Cornerstones: An Anthology
    of African American Literature. New York:
    St. Martin's, 1996.
```

Also list each selection by its author and title, followed by a cross-reference to the anthology, alphabeticing all entries.

```
Baker, Houston A., Jr. "There Is No More
     Beautiful Way." Donalson 856-63.

Ellison, Ralph. "What America Would Be Like
     without Blacks." Donalson 737-41.
```

11. TRANSLATION

Begin the entry with the author's name, and give the translator's name, preceded by *Trans.* ("Translated by"), after the title.

```
Zamora, Martha. Frida Kahlo: The Brush of
     Anguish. Trans. Marilyn Sode Smith. San
     Francisco: Chronicle, 1990.
```

If you cite a translated selection in an anthology, add *Trans.* and the translator's name before the title of the anthology.

```
Horace. The Art of Poetry. Trans. Smith Palmer
     Bovie. The Critical Tradition: Classic Texts
     and Contemporary Trends. Ed. David H.
     Richter. 2nd ed. Boston: Bedford, 1998.
     68-78.
```

12. EDITION OTHER THAN THE FIRST

Add the information, in abbreviated form, after the title.

```
Kelly, Alfred H., Winfred A. Harbison, and Herman
     Belz. The American Constitution: Its Origins
     and Development. 6th ed. New York: Norton,
     1983.
```

13. ONE VOLUME OF A MULTIVOLUME WORK

Give the volume number after the title, and list the number of volumes in the complete work after the date, using the abbreviations *Vol.* and *vols.*

```
Foner, Philip S., and Ronald L. Lewis, eds. The
    Black Worker. Vol. 3. Philadelphia:
    Lippincott, 1980. 8 vols.
```

14. TWO OR MORE VOLUMES OF A MULTIVOLUME WORK

Give the number of volumes in the complete work after the title, using the abbreviation *vols.*

```
Foner, Philip S., and Ronald L. Lewis, eds. The
    Black Worker. 8 vols. Philadelphia:
    Lippincott, 1980.
```

15. PREFACE, FOREWORD, INTRODUCTION, OR AFTERWORD

List the author of the item, the item title (not underlined, italicized, or in quotation marks), the title of the book, and its author's name, preceded by the word *By*. If the same person wrote both the book and the cited item, use just the last name after *By*. List the inclusive page numbers of the item at the end of the entry.

```
Schlesinger, Arthur M., Jr. Introduction. Pioneer
    Women: Voices from the Kansas Frontier. By
    Joanna L. Stratton. New York: Simon, 1981.
    11-15.
```

16. ENTRY IN A REFERENCE WORK

List the author of the entry, if known. If no author is identified, begin with the title. For a well-known work, just note any edition number and date after the name of the work. If the entries in the work are in alphabetical order, no volume or page numbers are needed.

```
"Hero." Merriam-Webster's Collegiate Dictionary.
     10th ed. 1996.

Johnson, Peder J. "Concept Learning."
     Encyclopedia of Education. 1971.
```

17. BOOK THAT IS PART OF A SERIES

Cite the series name as it appears on the title page, followed by any series number.

```
Moss, Beverly J., ed. Literacy across
     Communities. Written Lang. Ser. 2.
     Cresskill: Hampton, 1994.
```

18. REPUBLICATION

To cite a modern edition of an older book, add the original publication date, followed by a period, after the title.

```
Scott, Walter. Kenilworth. 1821. New York: Dodd,
     1956.
```

19. GOVERNMENT DOCUMENT

Begin with the author, if identified. If no author is given, start with the name of the government followed by the agency and any subdivision. Use abbreviations if they can be readily understood. Then list the title, underlined or italicized. For congressional documents, cite the number, session, house of Congress (using *S* for Senate and *H* or *HR* for House of Representatives), and the type (*Report, Resolution, Document*), in abbreviated form, and number of the material. If you cite the *Congressional Record,* give only the date and page number. Otherwise, end with the publication information; the publisher is often the Government Printing Office (*GPO*).

New Hampshire. Dept. of Transportation. Right of
     Way Salinity Reports, Hillsborough County,
     1985. Concord: New Hampshire Dept. of
     Transportation, 1986.

United States. Cong. House. Report of the Joint
     Subcommittee on Reconstruction. 39th Cong.,
     1st sess. H. Rept. 30. 1865. New York: Arno,
     1969.

United States. Census Bureau. Historical
     Statistics of the United States,
     Colonial Times to 1970. Washington: GPO,
     1975.

20. PAMPHLET

Treat a pamphlet as you would a book.

Why Is Central America a Conflict Area? Opposing
     Viewpoints Pamphlets. St. Paul: Greenhaven,
     1984.

21. PUBLISHED PROCEEDINGS OF A CONFERENCE

Treat proceedings as a book, but add information about the conference if it is not part of the title.

Martin, John Steven, and Christine Mason
     Sutherland, eds. Proceedings of the Canadian
     Society for the History of Rhetoric.
     Calgary, AB: Canadian Soc. for the History
     of Rhetoric, 1986.

MLA Format for a List of Works Cited   95

22. PUBLISHER'S IMPRINT

If a book was published by a publisher's imprint (indicated on the title page), hyphenate the imprint and the publisher's name.

```
Rose, Phyllis. Parallel Lives: Five Victorian
     Marriages. New York: Vintage-Random, 1984.
```

23. TITLE WITHIN THE TITLE

Do not underline or italicize the title of a book within the title of a book you are citing. Enclose in quotation marks the title of a short work within a book title, and underline or italicize it as you do the rest of the title.

```
Gilbert, Stuart. James Joyce's Ulysses. New York:
     Vintage-Random, 1955.

Renza, Louis A. "A White Heron" and the Question
     of a Minor Literature. Madison: U of
     Wisconsin P, 1984.
```

24. SACRED TEXT

To cite individual published editions of sacred books, begin the entry with the title, underlined or italicized. For versions of the Bible in which the version is not part of the title, list the version after the title. If your text does not specify a particular edition or version, the Bible and other sacred writings should not appear in the works-cited list.

```
The Jerusalem Bible. Garden City: Doubleday,
     1966.
```

Periodicals

The basic entry for a periodical includes three elements, each followed by a period.

- *Author.* List the author's last name first, followed by a comma and the first name.
- *Article title.* Enclose the title and any subtitle in quotation marks, and capitalize all major words. The closing period goes inside the closing quotation mark.
- *Publication information.* Give the periodical title (excluding any initial *A*, *An*, or *The*), underlined or italicized and with all major words capitalized; the volume number and issue number if appropriate; and the date of publication. For journals, list the year in parentheses followed by a colon, a space, and the inclusive page numbers. For magazines and newspapers, list the month (abbreviated, except for May, June, and July) or the day and month before the year, and do not use parentheses. Do not use *p.* or *pp.* before the page numbers. For inclusive page numbers, note all digits for numbers 1 to 99, and note only the last two digits and any others that change for numbers above 99 (*24–27, 134–45, 198–201*).

Here is an example of a basic entry for an article in a journal:

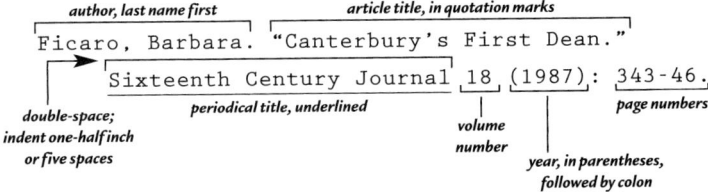

25. ARTICLE IN A JOURNAL PAGINATED BY VOLUME

Follow the journal title with the volume number in arabic numerals.

```
Norris, Margot. "Narration under a Blindfold:
    Reading Joyce's 'Clay.'" PMLA 102 (1987):
    206-15.
```

MLA Format for a List of Works Cited 97

26. ARTICLE IN A JOURNAL PAGINATED BY ISSUE

Put a period and the issue number after the volume number.

```
Loffy, John. "The Politics at Modernism's
     Funeral." Canadian Journal of Political and
     Social Theory 6.3 (1987): 89-96.
```

27. ARTICLE IN A MONTHLY MAGAZINE

Put the month (or months, hyphenated) before the year. Do not include volume or issue numbers.

```
Weiss, Philip. "The Book Thief: A True Tale of
     Bibliomania." Harper's Jan. 1994: 37-56.
```

28. ARTICLE IN A WEEKLY MAGAZINE

Include the day, month, and year in that order, with no commas between them. Do not include volume or issue numbers.

```
Daly, Steve. "Face to Face." Entertainment Weekly
     20 June 1997: 20-24.
```

29. ARTICLE IN A NEWSPAPER

Give the name of the newspaper, underlined or italicized, as it appears on the front page but without any initial *A, An,* or *The.* Add the city in brackets after the name if it is not part of the name. Then give the date and the edition (if listed), followed by a colon, a space, the section number or letter (if listed), and the page number(s). If the article appears on discontinuous pages, give the first page followed by a plus sign.

```
Vogel, Carol. "With Huge Gift, the Whitney Is No
     Longer a Poor Cousin." New York Times 3 Aug.
     2002, late ed.: A1+.
```

30. EDITORIAL OR LETTER TO THE EDITOR

Use the label *Editorial* or *Letter,* not underlined, italicized, or in quotation marks, after the title or after the author's name if there is no title.

```
Crews, Frederick. "Was Freud a Fraud?" Letter.
    New York Times Book Review 27 Mar. 1994: 27.
Magee, Doug. "Soldier's Home." Editorial. Nation
    26 Mar. 1988: 400-01.
```

31. UNSIGNED ARTICLE

Begin with the article title, alphabetizing the entry according to the first word after any initial *A, An,* or *The.*

```
"Tipping the Balance." Time 25 June 2001: 34+.
```

32. TWO OR MORE ARTICLES BY THE SAME AUTHOR(S)

Arrange the entries alphabetically by title. Include the name(s) of the author(s) in the first entry, but in subsequent entries use three hyphens followed by a period.

```
Safire, William. "Legit." New York Times Magazine
    14 Jan. 2001: 18.
---. "Off the Dime." New York Times Magazine 6
    Oct. 2002.
```

If you cite an article by one author who is also listed as the first coauthor of another article you cite, list the single-author article first, and repeat the author's name in the entry for the coauthored article. Also repeat the author's name if you cite an article in which that author is listed as the first of a different set of coauthors. Use three hyphens only when the article is by *exactly* the same author(s) as the previous entry.

33. REVIEW

List the reviewer's name and the title of the review, if any, followed by *Rev. of* and the title and author or director of the work reviewed. Then add the publication information for the periodical in which the review appears.

```
Solinger, Rickie. "Unsafe for Women." Rev. of
     Next Time, She'll Be Dead: Battering and How
     to Stop It, by Ann Jones. New York Times
     Book Review 20 Mar. 1994: 16.
```

34. ARTICLE WITH A TITLE WITHIN THE TITLE

Enclose in single quotation marks the title of a short work within an article title. Underline or italicize the title of a book within an article title.

```
Frey, Leonard H. "Irony and Point of View in
     'That Evening Sun.'" Faulkner Studies 2
     (1953): 33-40.
```

Electronic Sources

Electronic sources such as CD-ROMs, World Wide Web sites, and email differ from print sources in the ease with which they can be—and the frequency with which they are—changed, updated, or even eliminated. In addition, as the *MLA Handbook for Writers of Research Papers* notes, electronic media "so far lack agreed-on means of organizing works." In recommending the following guidelines for some of the most common kinds of electronic sources, the *Handbook* adds, "References to electronic works therefore must provide more information than print citations generally offer." Further guidelines for citing electronic sources can be found in the *Handbook* and online at <www.mla.org>.

For example, the most commonly cited electronic sources are documents from a Web site, such as essays, articles, or poems within a scholarly project, a reference database, a professional site, or an online periodical. The entry for such a source may include up to five basic elements, listed below, but always includes the last two:

- *Author.* List the author's last name first, followed by a comma and the first name. End with a period. If no author is given, begin the entry with the title.
- *Title.* Enclose the title and subtitle in quotation marks unless you are citing an entire site or an online book, which should be underlined or (if your instructor permits) italicized; capitalize all major words. End with a period inside the closing quotation marks.
- *Print publication information.* Give information about any previous or simultaneous publication pages, using the guidelines on pp. 76–78.
- *Electronic publication information.* List the following items, with a period after each one: the title of the site, underlined or italicized, with all major words capitalized; the editor(s) of the site, preceded by *Ed.*; the version number of the site, preceded by *Vers.*; the date of electronic publication or of the latest update, with the month, if any, abbreviated except for *May, June,* and *July*; and the name of any institution or organization that sponsors the site. (The sponsor's name usually appears at the bottom of the site's home page.)
- *Access information.* Give the most recent date you accessed the source and its URL, enclosed in angle brackets followed by a period. In general, give the complete URL for the work you are citing, including the opening *http, ftp, gopher, telnet,* or *news*. If the URL is very long and complicated, however, give the URL of the site's search page, if there is one, instead. If the site does not provide a usable URL for individual documents and citing the search page is inappropriate, give the URL of the site's home page; if a user can reach the document from the home page by clicking on a sequence of links, after the URL give the word *Path* followed by a colon and the sequence, with semicolons between the links and a period at the end. If the URL will not fit on one line, break it only after a slash, and do not add a hyphen at the break or allow your word-processing program to add one.

35. DOCUMENT FROM A WEB SITE

"France." Encyclopaedia Britannica Online. 2003.
    Encyclopaedia Britannica. 13 Mar. 2003
    <http://search.eb.com>.

"Important Dates in the Women's Rights Movement."
    History Channel.com. 2003. History Channel.
    13 Mar. 2003 <http://historychannel.com>.
    Path: Women's History; Special Feature—
    Women's Suffrage; The History of Women's
    Suffrage in America; Timeline.

Scott, Walter. "Remarks on Frankenstein, or the
    Modern Prometheus: A Novel." Romantic
    Circles. Ed. Neil Fraistat, Steven Jones,
    Donald Reiman, and Carl Stahmer. 1996. 15
    Apr. 1998 <http://www.udel.edu/swilson/mws/
    bemrev.html>.

36. ENTIRE WEB SITE

Follow the guidelines for a specific document but begin with the title of the site and the name of the editor(s), if any.

The Orlando Project: An Integrated History of
    Women's Writing in the British Isles. 1997.
    U of Alberta. 9 Oct. 1997
    <http://www.ualberta.ca/ORLANDO/>.

Weather.com. 2003. Weather Channel Interactive.
    13 Mar. 2003 <http://www.weather.com>.

37. COURSE, DEPARTMENT, OR PERSONAL SITE

For the Web site of an academic course, give the name of the instructor, the title of the course, a description such as *Course home page*, the dates of the course, the name of the department, the name of the institution, and the access information. For the site of an academic department, give the name of the department, such as *English*; a description such as *Dept. home page*; the name of the institution; and the access information. Put a period after each item, and do not underline or italicize any items or enclose them in quotation marks.

```
Lunsford, Andrea A. Memory and Media. Course home
     page. Sept.-Dec. 2002. Dept. of English,
     Stanford U. 13 Mar. 2003 <http://www.
     stanford.edu/class/english12sc>.
```

For a personal site, include the name of the person who created it; the title, underlined or italicized, or (if there is no title) a description such as *Home page*; the date of the last update, if given; and the access information.

```
Lunsford, Andrea A. Home page. 15 Mar. 2003. 17
     Mar. 2003 <http://www.stanford.edu/
     ~lunsfor1/>.
```

38. ONLINE BOOK

Begin with the name of the author or, if only an editor, a compiler, or a translator is identified, the name of that person followed by a comma and *ed., comp.,* or *trans.* Then give the title, underlined or italicized, and the name of any editor, compiler, or translator not listed earlier, preceded by *Ed., Comp.,* or *Trans.* Include any publication information (city, publisher, and year) for the print version that is given, and end with the date of access and the URL, in angle brackets.

```
Riis, Jacob A. How the Other Half Lives: Studies
     among the Tenements of New York. Ed. David
     Phillips. New York: Scribner's, 1890. 26
     Mar. 1998 <http://www.cis.yale.edu/amstud/
     inforev/riis/title.html>.
```

If a book is part of a scholarly project or similar site, after the information about the print version give the information about the project (title, editor, version number, date, and sponsor). If you are citing a poem, essay, or other short work within a book, include its title, in quotation marks, after the author's name. Give the URL of the short work, not of the book, if they differ.

```
Dickinson, Emily. "The Grass." Poems: Emily
     Dickinson. Boston, 1891. Humanities Text
     Initiative American Verse Collection. Ed.
     Nancy Kushigian. 1995. U of Michigan. 9 Oct.
     1997 <http://www.planet.net/pkrisxle/emily/
     poemsOnline.html>.
```

39. ONLINE GOVERNMENT DOCUMENT

Cite an online government document as you would a printed government work, adding the electronic publication information, the date of access, and the URL, in angle brackets.

```
United States. Environmental Protection Agency.
     Office of Emergency and Remedial Response.
     This Is Superfund. Jan. 2000. 16 Aug. 2002
     <http://www.epa.gov/superfund/whatissf/
     sfguide.htm>.
```

40. ARTICLE IN AN ONLINE PERIODICAL

To cite an article in an online scholarly journal, magazine, or newspaper, follow the guidelines given on pages 96–99 for citing articles in print periodicals, but adapt them as necessary to the online medium. Include the author's name; the title, in quotation marks; the name of the periodical, underlined or italicized; the volume, issue, or other identifying number, if any; the date of publication; the range or total number of pages, paragraphs, parts, or other sections, if they are numbered; the date of access; and the URL, in angle brackets.

```
Browning, Tonya. "Embedded Visuals: Student
     Design in Web Spaces." Kairos: A Journal for
     Teachers of Writing 2.1 (1997). 9 Oct. 1997
     <http://english.ttu.edu/kairos/current/
     toc.html>.
Gallagher, Brian. "Greta Garbo Is Sad: Some
     Historical Reflections on the Paradoxes of
     Stardom in the American Film Industry, 1910-
     1960." Images: A Journal of Film and Popular
     Culture 3 (1997): 7 pts. 7 Aug. 2000
     <http://imagesjournal.com/issue03/
     infocus.htm>.
Gawande, Atul. "Drowsy Docs." Slate. 9 Oct. 1997.
     10 Oct. 1997 <http://www.slate.com/
     MedicalExaminer/97-10-09/MedicalExaminer
     .asp>.
```

41. WORK FROM AN ONLINE SUBSCRIPTION SERVICE

To cite a work from an online subscription service, such as America Online or Lexis-Nexis, follow the guidelines on pages 102–4 for the appropriate type of work, such as an article in an online periodical. If possible, end the entry with the URL of the specific work or, if it is very long and complicated, the URL of the service's search page. If, however, the service supplies no URL or one that is not accessible to other subscribers or after the current session, you will need to provide other access information.

If you used a personal subscription service to access a source, include the name of the service before the date of access. After the date, depending on the service's retrieval system, then give either the word *Keyword* followed by a colon and the keyword you used or the word *Path* followed by a colon and the sequence of links you followed, with semicolons between the links.

```
Weeks, W. William. "Beyond the Ark." Nature
     Conservancy Mar.-Apr. 1999. America Online.
     2 Apr. 1999. Keyword: Ecology.
```

If you accessed the service through a library's subscription, after the information about the work give the name of the database, underlined or italicized, if you know it; the name of the service; the library; the date of access; and the URL of the service's home page, in angle brackets, if you know it.

```
Croal, N'Gai. "Games Look to Hip-Hop." Newsweek
     12 May 2003: 34. Lexis-Nexis. Newman Lib.,
     Baruch Coll., 27 May 2003 <https://
     web.lexis-nexis.com/universe>.

Gordon, Andrew. "It's Not Such a Wonderful
     Life: The Neurotic George Bailey." American
     Journal of Psychoanalysis 54.3 (1994):
     219-33. PsycINFO. EBSCO. City U of New York,
     Graduate Center Lib. 26 Oct. 2003
     <http://www.epnet.com>.
```

42. POSTING TO A DISCUSSION GROUP

In citing an online posting, begin with the author's name; the title of the document, in quotation marks; the description *Online posting*, not underlined or italicized or in quotation marks; and the date of posting. For a listserv posting, then give the name of the listserv; the date of access; and the URL of the listserv or the email address of its moderator or supervisor. Always cite an archival version of the posting if possible.

```
Chagall, Nancy. "Web Publishing and Censorship."
     Online posting. 2 Feb. 1997. ACW: The
     Alliance for Computers and Writing
     Discussion List. 10 Oct. 1997
     <http://english.ttu.edu/acw-1/archive.htm>.
```

For a posting to a newsgroup, end with the date of access and the name of the newsgroup, in angle brackets, with the prefix *news*.

```
Martin, Jerry. "The IRA and Sinn Fein." Online
     posting. 31 Mar. 1998. 1 Apr. 1998
     <news:soc.culture.irish>.
```

43. EMAIL

Include the writer's name; the subject line of the message, in quotation marks; a description of the message that mentions the recipient; and the date of the message.

```
Lunsford, Andrea A. "New Texts." Email to Kristin
     Bowen. 25 July 2002.
```

44. SYNCHRONOUS COMMUNICATION

In citing a posting in a forum such as a MOO, MUD, or IRC, include the name(s) of any specific speaker(s) you are citing; a description of the event; its date; the name of the forum; the date of access; and the URL, with the prefix *telnet.* Always cite an archival version of the posting if possible.

```
Patuto, Jeremy, Simon Fennel, and James Goss. The
     Mytilene Debate. 9 May 1996. MiamiMOO. 28
     Mar. 1998 <http://moo.cas.muohio.edu/
     cgi-bin/moo?look+4085>.
```

45. OTHER ELECTRONIC SOURCES

In citing other kinds of electronic sources, follow the guidelines given on pages 100–7, but adapt them as necessary to the electronic medium. Here are examples of citations for a photograph of a work of art, an interview, and a film, accessed online.

```
Aleni, Giulio. K'un-yu t'u-shu. ca. 1620.
     Vatican, Rome. Rome Reborn: The Vatican
     Library and Renaissance Culture. May 1993.
     28 Mar. 2003 <http://archive.ncsa.uiuc.edu/
     SDG/Experimental/vatican.exhibit/exhibit/
     full-images/i-rome_to_china/china02.gif>.

Dyson, Esther. Interview. Hotseat 23 May 1997
     <http://www.hotwired.com/packet/hotseat/
     97/20/index4a.html>.

The Godfather. Dir. Francis Ford Coppola.
     28 Mar. 1998 <http://UK.imdbj.com/
     Title?Godfather,+The+[1972]>.
```

46. PERIODICALLY REVISED DATABASE ON CD-ROM

Include the author's name; publication information for the print version of the text (including its title and date of publication); the title of the database, underlined or italicized; the medium (*CD-ROM*); the name of the company producing it; and the electronic publication date (month and year, if possible).

```
Natchez, Gladys. "Frida Kahlo and Diego Rivera:
     The Transformation of Catastrophe to
     Creativity." Psychotherapy-Patient 4.1
     (1987): 153-74. PsycLIT. CD-ROM.
     SilverPlatter. Nov. 1994.
```

47. SINGLE-ISSUE CD-ROM, DISKETTE, OR MAGNETIC TAPE

Before the place of publication, include the medium and, if appropriate, the number of the electronic edition, release, or version. If you are citing only a part of the source, end with the page, paragraph, screen, or other section numbers of the part if they are indicated in the source—either the range of numbers (*pp. 78–83*) or, if each section is numbered separately, the total number of sections in the part (*8 screens*).

```
"Communion." The Oxford English Dictionary. 2nd
     ed. CD-ROM. Oxford: Oxford UP, 1992.
```

48. MULTIDISC CD-ROM

Include either the total number of discs or, if you use material from only one, the number of that disc.

```
The 1998 Grolier Multimedia Encyclopedia. CD-ROM.
     2 discs. Danbury: Grolier Interactive, 1997.
The 1998 Grolier Multimedia Encyclopedia. CD-ROM.
     Disc 2. Danbury: Grolier Interactive, 1997.
```

49. WORK IN AN INDETERMINATE MEDIUM

If you are not sure whether material accessed through a local electronic network is stored on the central computer's hard drive or on a

CD-ROM, use the label *Electronic*. Include any publication information that is available, the name of the network or of its sponsoring organization, and the date of access.

> "Communion." <u>The Oxford English Dictionary</u>. 2nd
> ed. Oxford: Oxford UP, 1992. Electronic.
> OhioLink, Ohio State U Lib. 15 Apr. 1998.

50. SOFTWARE OR COMPUTER PROGRAM

Include the title, underlined or italicized; the version number; and the publication information. If you are citing software that was downloaded, replace the publication information with the date of access and the URL, in angle brackets.

> <u>McAfee Office 2000</u>. Vers. 2.0. Santa Clara:
> Network Associates, 1999.

Other Kinds of Sources

51. UNPUBLISHED DISSERTATION OR THESIS

Enclose the title in quotation marks. Add the identification *Diss.* or *MA thesis, MS thesis,* and so on; the name of the university or professional school, a comma, and the year the dissertation or thesis was accepted.

> LeCourt, Donna. "The Self in Motion: The Status
> of the (Student) Subject in Composition
> Studies." Diss. Ohio State U, 1993.

52. PUBLISHED DISSERTATION

Cite a published dissertation as a book, adding the identification *Diss.* and the name of the university. If the dissertation was published by University Microfilms International, add *Ann Arbor: UMI,* and the year, and list the UMI number at the end of the entry.

> Botts, Roderic C. <u>Influences in the Teaching of
> English, 1917-1935: An Illusion of Progress</u>.

Diss. Northeastern U, 1970. Ann Arbor: UMI,
1971. 71-1799.

53. ARTICLE FROM A MICROFORM

Treat the article as a printed work, but add the name of the microform—printed material reduced in size, such as microfiche—and information for locating it.

Sharpe, Lora. "A Quilter's Tribute." Boston Globe
25 Mar. 1989. Newsbank: Social Relations 12
(1989): fiche 6, grids B4-6.

54. INTERVIEW

List the person interviewed and then the title of the interview, if any, in quotation marks (or underlined or italicized if the interview is a complete work). If the interview has no title, use the label *Interview* (not underlined, italicized, or in quotation marks), and identify the source. If you were the interviewer, use the label *Telephone interview, Personal interview,* or *Email interview.* End with the date(s) the interview took place.

Beja, Morris. Personal interview. 2 Oct. 2002.
Schorr, Daniel. Interview. Weekend Edition. Natl.
    Public Radio. WEVO, Concord. 26 Mar. 1988.

55. LETTER

If the letter was published, cite it as a selection in a book, noting the date and any identifying number after the title.

Frost, Robert. "Letter to Editor of the
    Independent." 28 Mar. 1894. Selected Letters
    of Robert Frost. Ed. Lawrance Thompson. New
    York: Holt, 1964. 19.

If the letter was sent to you, follow this form:

Anzaldúa, Gloria. Letter to the author. 10 Sept.
    2002.

56. FILM, VIDEO, OR DVD

In general, start with the title, underlined or italicized; then name the director; the company distributing the film, videocassette, or DVD; and the date of its release. Other contributors, such as writers or actors, may follow the director. If you cite a particular person's work, start the entry with that person's name. For a videocassette or DVD, include the original film release date (if relevant) and the label *Videocassette* or *DVD*.

Face/Off. Dir. John Woo. Perf. John Travolta and
    Nicolas Cage. Paramount, 1997.
The Star. Dir. Lawrence Pitkethly. Videocassette.
    CBS/Fox Video, 1995.
Weaver, Sigourney, perf. Aliens. Dir. James
    Cameron. 20th Century Fox, 1986.

57. TELEVISION OR RADIO PROGRAM

In general, begin with the title of the program, underlined or italicized. Then list the narrator, director, actors, or other contributors, as necessary; the network; the local station and city, if any; and the broadcast date. If you cite a particular person's work, begin the entry with that person's name. If you cite a particular episode, include any title, in quotation marks, before the program's title. If the program is part of a series, include the series title (not underlined, italicized, or in quotation marks) before the network.

Box Office Bombshell: Marilyn Monroe. Writ. Andy
    Thomas, Jeff Schefel, and Kevin Burns. Dir.

```
            Bill Harris. Narr. Peter Graves. A&E
            Biography. Arts and Entertainment Network.
            23 Oct. 2002.
Gellar, Sarah Michelle, perf. "Once More, with
      Feeling." Buffy the Vampire Slayer. Dir.
      Joss Whedon. WB. WWOR. New York. 6 Nov.
      2001.
```

58. SOUND RECORDING

Begin with the name of the composer, performer, or conductor, depending on whose work you are citing. Next give the title of the recording, which is underlined or italicized, or the title of the composition, which is not. End with the manufacturer, a comma, and the year of issue. If you are not citing a compact disc, give the medium before the manufacturer. If you are citing a particular song, include its title, in quotation marks, before the title of the recording.

```
Grieg, Edvard. Concerto in A minor, op. 16. Cond.
      Eugene Ormandy. Philadelphia Orch. LP. RCA,
      1989.
Kilcher, Jewel. "Amen." Pieces of You. A&R, 1994.
```

59. WORK OF ART OR PHOTOGRAPH

List the artist or photographer (if available); the work's title, underlined or italicized; the name of the museum or other location; and the city. If you want to include the date the work was created, add it after the title.

```
Kahlo, Frida. Self-Portrait with Cropped Hair.
      1940. Museum of Mod. Art, New York.
```

To cite a photograph or reproduction of a work—a work you have not seen in person—add the publication information for the source where the photograph appears.

Peale, Charles Wilson. The Artist in His Museum.
    1822. Philadelphia Acad. of the Fine Arts.
    Adcult USA: The Triumph of Advertising in
    American Culture. By James B. Twitchell.
    New York: Columbia UP, 1996. 214.

60. LECTURE OR SPEECH

List the speaker, the title in quotation marks, the name of the sponsoring institution or group, the place, and the date. If the speech is untitled, use a label such as *Lecture* or *Keynote speech*.

Lu, Min-Zhan. "The Politics of Listening."
    Conf. on Coll. Composition and
    Communication. Palmer House, Chicago.
    3 Apr. 1998.

61. PERFORMANCE

List the title, underlined or italicized, other appropriate details (such as composer, writer, director), the place, and the date. If you cite a particular person's work, begin the entry with that person's name.

Frankie and Johnny in the Clair de Lune. By
    Terrence McNally. Dir. Paul Benedict.
    Westside Arts Theater, New York.
    18 Jan. 1988.

62. MAP OR CHART

Cite a map or chart as you would a book with an unknown author, adding the label *Map* or *Chart*.

Pennsylvania. Map. Chicago: Rand, 1985.

63. CARTOON OR COMIC STRIP

List the artist's name, the title of the work (if it has one), in quotation marks; *Cartoon* or *Comic Strip;* and the usual publication information.

```
Trudeau, Garry. "Doonesbury." Comic Strip.
    Philadelphia Inquirer 9 Mar. 1988: 37.
```

64. ADVERTISEMENT

Name the item or organization being advertised, add the label *Advertisement,* and then supply the standard information about the source in which the ad appears.

```
Dannon Yogurt. Advertisement. TV Guide 4 Dec.
    1999: A14.
```

A Student Research Essay, MLA Style

The writer of the following essay, Shannan Palma, responded to an assignment for an introductory writing class that asked her to choose a subject she found of interest and "use it as the basis of a research essay that makes and substantiates a claim." In response to questions, Shannan Palma's instructor clarified some requirements of the assignment: the essay should use information from both print and online sources to support the claim, it should be roughly ten to fifteen pages in length, and it should be written for members of the writing class. In preparing the essay, Shannan Palma followed the MLA guidelines described here. She was required to submit a formal outline in addition to the final essay. Note that we have reproduced the essay in a narrower (and longer) format than you will have on a standard ($8\frac{1}{2}'' \times 11''$) sheet of paper.

Palma 1

Shannan Palma
Professor Lunsford
English 167
18 November 2002

   Hollywood and the Hero: Outline

Thesis statement: Recent films strongly suggest that the hero of the twenty-first century will most likely appear not as a Hollywood star or a mythical manifestation but as a combination of mortal and machine--in short, a cyborg.

I. Originally relying on earlier heroes from the realms of myth and history, Hollywood studios gradually developed a system for transforming actors into star-heroes.
  A. Moviegoers began to identify a favorite hero-character with the particular actor who played him or her.
  B. The studios recognized the financial possibilities of the mass idolization of a commercialized hero and set out to manufacture this "product" efficiently.
    1. The persona that a studio developed to turn an actor into a star was the only public identity that actor was allowed to have.

2. Early examples of the star-hero included Douglas Fairbanks and Mary Pickford.
II. As the studio system disintegrated in the 1950s and 1960s, and the stars lost the publicity shield it had provided, the problems of stardom became obvious to the public.
   A. Films from this period show that the movie industry was self-mockingly aware of its pitfalls.
      1. <u>Sunset Boulevard</u> showed what happened when a hero-image was no longer popular and the system abandoned the star it had made.
      2. <u>A Star Is Born</u> showed how the system created a perfect image and forced a human being to become it.
   B. Widely publicized scandals like that surrounding the death of Marilyn Monroe further increased the public's knowledge of star-hero failings.
   C. Although scandals seemed only to increase public adoration of stars by giving their images an air of tragic martyrdom, public perception of star-heroes as <u>ideals</u> began to fade.

III. More recent decades have seen the confusion of identity between film characters and stars take a new form, which has further contributed to the decline of the hero.
   A. The last vestiges of the studio system's image-projection and -protection have vanished, leaving the public with few illusions about the lives of star-heroes.
   B. Rather than admire stars for their heroic achievements and personal qualities, the public envies them for their lifestyle.
   C. Profound cynicism toward the hero as ideal is reflected in films such as The Ref, which encourage audiences to identify heroes with the stars that portray them rather than vice versa.
   D. The disappearance of the hero-ideal in film has led to a lack of lasting empathy with the hero among movie audiences.
      1. After audiences see a movie, they no longer associate the character with the film, but rather the actor with the film.
      2. To re-create that lasting empathy in a modern context, we need heroes who can overcome the problem of mistaken

Palma 4

        identity and who are believable and relevant to today's world.
IV. The 1997 film Face/Off can serve as one prototype for overcoming these obstacles.
    A. The film turns mistaken identity against itself, with the two lead actors switching roles in such a way that the audience has its preconceptions of the relationships between star and character challenged and develops a lasting empathy with the hero.
    B. With its portrayal of a hero who resorts to advanced technology to take on the face of his enemy, the film also provides a prototype for the cyborg hero, a form that the twenty-first-century hero may take.

Shannan Palma

Professor Lunsford

English 167

18 November 2002

        Hollywood and the Hero:

   Solving a Case of Mistaken Identity

In the song "Amen" from the best-selling album Pieces of You, Jewel Kilcher poses questions about heroes that are worth asking.

> Where are my angels?
> Where's my golden one?
> Where's my hope
> Now that my heroes
> have gone?

These questions are important because the hero, what Merriam-Webster's Collegiate Dictionary defines as "a man admired for his achievements and noble qualities" ("Hero," def. 1c), seems to have vanished from American popular culture. From Hercules to Robin Hood, from Joan of Arc to Scarlett O'Hara, male and female heroes alike have reflected the ideals and the most admired traits of their respective times: brute strength or sharply honed cunning, devotion to duty or desire for rebellion. Throughout history, and specifically U.S. history, the hero-ideal has

Palma 2

endured in the arts--until now. The twentieth century, which started off with the promising evolution of the hero from figure of legend and literature to star of the silver screen, seems to have ended with the near death of the hero as ideal in popular culture.

The eclipse of the hero in film results from a case of what may be called "mistaken identity," which has caused film heroes' fates to become inextricably intertwined with the fates of the actors who portray them. This research essay will explore whether today's films truly signal the end of the hero-ideal and preview a hero-less future, or whether they instead help the hero evolve to a different, perhaps more realistic, level. If the latter is true, the question then becomes one of what form the new hero will take onscreen. This essay will argue that recent films strongly suggest that the hero of the twenty-first century will most likely appear not as a Hollywood star or a mythical manifestation but as a combination of mortal and machine--in short, a cyborg.[1]

Before either of these questions can be addressed, however, a brief history of Hollywood's relationship with the hero is necessary. Our heroes once came primarily from the fantasy of myth and the remove of history and literature. King Arthur, the Three Musketeers, Jo March of <u>Little Women</u>, Annie Oakley--all have spent time on the hero's pedestal. With the development of motion pictures in the early twentieth century, many of these heroes made the transition from legend to life, or at least to life on the screen. Soon moviegoers were able not only to read about and imagine their heroes in action but also to see them in the most glamorous incarnations Hollywood could create. Fans began to identify a favorite hero-character with the particular actor who played him or her, and this burgeoning case of mistaken identity did not go unnoticed for long. Film historian Morris Beja notes that although the studios, then the most powerful force in Hollywood, had originally hoped to give actors as little influence as possible over the studios' operations, it quickly became obvious that "movie stars sold tickets." Recognizing the enormous financial possibilities inherent in the mass idolization of a commercialized hero, the industry set out to manufacture this "product" as efficiently as possible. As a 1995 video on the star system in Hollywood explains:

> In the old days of the studio system there was a structure for developing stars. Players were owned body and soul, signed to long-term contracts. With the powerful publicity machine run by the studio they could reach an audience of millions. But that alone did not guarantee success. The problem for the studio was to find the one persona out of many possible character roles that would boost a character to stardom. (The Star)

Studios found that manufacturing movie stars was not easy. It required an actor with just the right combination of style, charisma, and talent, and it required just the right roles and public persona to make that actor a star. When it succeeded, however, the mistaken identity was complete. The star became an icon--an ideal--a hero. Many fictional hero types (such as the romantic hero and the western hero) carried over from the prefilm era; but new kinds of heroes also emerged, identified even more closely by the public with the stars who originated them. Early examples of the star-hero included silent film stars Douglas Fairbanks and Mary Pickford. "The swashbuckler was born with . . . Fairbanks," according to Beja, who also sees Pickford as the prototype of the brave or "plucky" movie heroine. As Richard deCordova notes in a memorable phrase, the studios wanted to convince millions of moviegoers that "the real hero behave[d] just like the reel hero" (qtd. in Gallagher, pt. 2). Therefore, the persona that a studio developed to turn a working actor into a star was the only public identity that actor would be allowed to have. Film historians like Beja and deCordova, who explores this topic in his book <u>Picture Personalities: The Emergence of the Star System in America</u>, say that the public's conceptual link between the hero and the star is the reason studios tried so hard to encourage the idea that stars like Fairbanks and Pickford had no private personalities separate from those of their onscreen characters. (See Fig. 1.)

As silent films gave way to "talkies" and Hollywood cinema emerged as a cultural force in and of itself, new names replaced those of Fairbanks and Pickford on theater marquees. The star system, however, only grew more deeply

Palma 6

entrenched. As long as the star-hero stayed separate from the public, buffered by studios in order to keep the image intact, his or her fictional self remained safe. But the strain of living up to a legend instead of living a life took a toll on the private, "real" selves. Brian Gallagher cites a remark by Cary Grant that sums up the strain many stars must have felt: "Everybody wants to be Cary Grant. Even I want to be Cary Grant" (pt. 3). As the studio system disintegrated in the 1950s and the 1960s and the stars lost the publicity shield it had provided, this toll became glaringly obvious to their adoring public.

Films from this period show that the movie industry was self-mockingly aware of its pitfalls. Sunset Boulevard, released in 1950, showed what happened when a hero-image was no longer profitable and the system abandoned the star it had made. Gloria Swanson played the fictional silent film star Norma Desmond, once young and adored, now aging and forgotten, who tries in vain to recapture her lost glory and ends her quest in tragedy. A Star Is Born, remade in 1954 with Judy Garland in the lead role, chronicled the rise of a young woman from nobody

Fig. 1. Baron De Meyer, Mary Pickford, circa 1915, MPTV Images, Los Angeles. Hollywood studios tried to stage-manage the image of stars like Mary Pickford to create public illusions of heroic, almost mythological beings.

to star, showing the reality of how the system created a perfect image and forced a human being to become it (Corey and Ochoa 353, 347). Yet even though these films showed the artificiality and destructiveness of the star system, at the same time they helped to perpetuate it. After all, the fictional star was played by a real-life one--and thus fiction and truth became even further intertwined.

Approximately a decade later, in 1962, Marilyn Monroe died of what was officially ruled an accidental overdose of sleeping pills. And in the words of a television biography, "almost instantly, the lurid circumstances of [her] death made national headlines around the world . . . . Marilyn Monroe was dead. Marilyn the Myth was born" (Box Office Bombshell). The supposedly idyllic life stars lived was being steadily exposed as false through both fictional tragedies and actual scandals, yet paradoxically the public did not turn against the stars but only focused their fascination in a slightly different way. Singer and songwriter Elton John immortalized the unique cult of fame that overshadowed Monroe's death in his 1973 song "Candle in the Wind," when he wrote of his own youthful feelings toward her: "Your candle burned out long before/Your legend ever did."[2] Rather than serving to separate the hero from the star, in fact, scandals only bound the two more closely together, lending a tragic, martyred cast to the star's image. The public's adoration of their stars did not diminish. Their perception of their heroes as ideals, however, began to fade.

Fast forward from the fifties and sixties to the present: forty to fifty years later. A brief excerpt from the celebrity gossip-fest Hollywood Confidential shows that the last vestiges of the studio system's image-projection and -protection have vanished:

> Well into the throes of drug addiction by the time she was thirteen, Drew Barrymore attempted suicide by cutting her wrists with a kitchen knife.
>
> Rosemary Clooney was addicted to prescription drugs and, after two embattled marriages to José Ferrer, was admitted to a psych ward.
>
> Francis Ford Coppola takes lithium.
>
> Patty (Call Me Anna) Duke is a manic-depressive. (Amende 247)

No longer do stars try to hide their personal lives from the public, and every scandal, every lie is exposed in the short run. Thus today's public holds very few illusions about the lives of their star-heroes. Although stars are still "living heroes," the relationship between the two terms has changed: rather than admiring stars for their heroic achievements and personal qualities, the public simply envies them for their lifestyle--their immense power, wealth, and fame. Even after the real-life heroism of September 11, a profound cynicism persists toward the hero as ideal, and this cynicism is reflected in the portrayal of the fictional hero in current American films. It is a portrayal that perpetuates the problem of mistaken identity noted earlier, but in reverse, with heroes being identified with the stars that portray them, rather than vice versa.

The 1994 film <u>The Ref</u> offers a fairly recent example of this reversal and of the cynicism it both grows out of and feeds into. As a review on the ABC News Web site <u>Mr. Showbiz</u> notes:

> Judy Davis and Kevin Spacey are a married couple who for the life of them can't stop bickering. Denis Leary is the burglar who's taken them hostage on Christmas Eve. Writers Marie Weiss and Richard LaGravanese have built a . . . platform . . . from which <u>Leary can freely launch himself into the mad stand-up monologues of outrage and spleen that are his trademark</u> [emphasis mine]. (Feeney)

A closer look at this film tells us more. It is
Christmas Eve, a traditional time of sharing and
harmony among loved ones, yet the married couple
in the film and the relatives who descend upon
them for the holidays are all so bitter,
sarcastic, and self-absorbed that even a hardened
criminal is appalled by them. As the values
associated with Christmas are turned on their ear
and exposed as empty vanity in today's society,
the criminal becomes a cynical sort of antihero:
unlike his hostages, he at least remembers what a
family is supposed to act like. The film's
message was emphasized by the casting of comedian
Leary in the title role, casting that capitalized
on his reputation as a one-man mouthpiece for the
Middle-American cynicism or anti-ideals of the
nineties. The fictional commentary of Leary's
character was made more believable to the
audience because the majority of them were
familiar with its similarities to the actual
commentary made famous by Leary himself. Rather
than the hero creating the star, the star now
forms the hero.

  The disappearance of the hero-ideal as a
separate entity from, or as a model for, the star
has led to a second and perhaps more complex

Palma 12

problem: with most modern films, there is a peculiar absence of lasting empathy of the audience with the hero. Apart from the rare phenomenon such as Luke Skywalker in Star Wars (1977), not only do modern movie heroes not exist apart from actors in audiences' minds, but they do not stay there for long. Think of Sigourney Weaver as Ripley, savior of humanity from Aliens (1986), Mel Gibson as a Revolutionary War soldier in The Patriot (2000), or Will Smith as an alien-hunting secret agent in Men in Black II (2002). In fact, this wording reveals just how most moviegoers do think of those heroes--the roles are indistinguishable from the stars--and after audiences see a movie, they no longer associate the character and the film, but rather the actor and the film. The difference between the short shelf life of modern heroes and the staying power of their old-style predecessors is evident if we look at film remakes of novels like Little Women and The Three Musketeers, in which the characters do supersede the actors in importance. But such films only cater to audience nostalgia for the time when those heroes gave cause for belief and hope, when the culture on which they were based held some ideals. These classic heroes may endure in memory, but they will never again have the mythic power that they did once upon a time. To re-create that lasting empathy in a modern context, we need films that can overcome mistaken identity and that contain heroes who are believable and relevant to today's world. Fortunately, in 1997 such a film, and such a hero, came to the screen.

Think of the current film hero as, to borrow a term from The Princess Bride (1987), "mostly dead." Not having died, the hero needs not rebirth but revival or regeneration. To begin regenerating the hero, then, it is necessary to overcome (1) the audience's preconceptions about the stars' relationships to the characters they play, and (2) the failure of recent hero-characters to invoke a lasting empathy in the public. The 1997 film Face/Off can serve as one prototype for overcoming both of these obstacles and thus for resolving once and for all the problem of mistaken identity.

First, the plot and characterization of this film provide an opportunity to prove that it is possible for a character to exist and be identified apart from the star who plays him or her. During the course of the story, the two main

Palma 14

characters, hero Sean Archer and villain Castor
Troy, undergo surgery that exchanges their faces.
The two stars of the film start off playing
particular characters, John Travolta as Archer
and Nicolas Cage as Troy; but approximately
twenty minutes into the film they switch roles.
(See Fig. 2.) In an interview for a magazine
article, Travolta described his take on imitating
his costar:

> [Cage's walk is] a saunter almost. It's
> very specific to Nick's natural gait.
> And I said if you don't mind, maybe we
> could use that Nick Cage cadence for
> the bad guy's voice, too, and I could
> just adapt that. You know, the way Nick
> slows down and enunciates and
> pronunciates. He's almost poetic in his
> talking. (qtd. in Daly 24)

Director John Woo and others involved in the
making of Face/Off seem to have used audience
preconceptions about actor-idiosyncrasies being
identical to character-idiosyncrasies, purposely
emphasized in the beginning of the film, to make
the switch-off of actors and roles that much more
shocking and real to the audience. They turned
mistaken identity against itself. Moviegoers who

Palma 15

Fig. 2. Stephen Vaughan, Nicolas Cage and John Travolta in Face/Off, 1997, Photofest, New York. The actors switched roles partway through Face/Off, a technique that helped audiences see their characters as figures independent of the actors portraying them.

had seen Cage and Travolta act before, who associated their faces with their body language, found that when the body language remained the same, even with a new face, it was convincing. This disassociation of actor from character negates the second obstacle to regeneration of the hero as well. Without mistaken identity to cloud the issue, Archer was able to create a lasting empathy with the audience. Even after the audience left the darkness of the theater, his

Palma 16

character could not be viewed on anything but its own terms.

In 2000, John Woo touched on the theme of mistaken identity again in Mission: Impossible II. Rogue agent Sean Ambrose steals the identity of Ethan Hunt (Tom Cruise) at several points in the film, using technology and elaborate disguises. In these few scenes, Tom Cruise shrugs off some of the actor-idiosyncrasies he plays up throughout the rest of the film.

With the complex problem of mistaken identity overcome, what remains is to create a believable hero who is relevant to today's world. In this context, the major challenge is that the model for the old hero, in Western culture at least, is based on the view that a human being is essentially a unified organic whole and can be labeled in some way: as epic hero, romantic hero, tragic hero, swashbuckling hero, western hero, detective hero, and so on. In the contemporary world, we can no longer believe in such a one-dimensional being. In one of the essays in her anthology Simians, Cyborgs, and Women, historian of science Donna J. Haraway claims that our dreams of organic unity and coherence are futile. In their place, she recommends the cyborg figure, which can give us a new dream of ourselves as multiple, surpassing either body or machine (181). In fact, Haraway argues that with our thinking computers, our routine organ transplants and high-technology prostheses, human beings in the late twentieth century were already living in a world of cyborgs--"hybrid[s] of machine and organism, [creatures] of social reality as well as [creatures] of fiction" (149). Much of Haraway's analysis can be applied to the emerging film hero.

The reel hero can no longer exist as a contained organic whole in today's fractured, technology-driven society. The human aspect of the hero has been damaged by mistaken identity to the extent that moviegoers will no longer put an extraordinary amount of faith in it. They no longer want the lie of static perfection given by classic heroes such as Hercules or Robin Hood and betrayed by film stars of Monroe's, and later Barrymore's, generations, but neither will a hero as openly damaged as such stars suffice in and of itself. Within their realistic heroes, people still want to hold firm to a core of something untainted by human frailties. At just this moment, the cyborg hero has emerged in film.

Again, Face/Off offers a useful demonstration. The character of Archer, a tortured FBI agent who spends years tracking the criminal (Troy) who gunned down his little boy, is not a hero, in the classic sense of the word, nor is he an antihero, in the modern sense of the word. Instead, he is a prototype for the emerging twenty-first-century hero, a figure whose humanity is not perfect but rather is damaged beyond repair (like the American culture's belief in the hero-ideal). To defeat "evil," Archer must use technology to "become" his enemy--literally wear his face and take his place in the world. As Janice Rushing and Thomas Frentz put it in their book Projecting the Shadow: The Cyborg Hero in American Film, "to survive, a man must be technological, and to thrive, he must be technologically adept" (147). The new heroes cannot be sustained without the props of the modern world. Technology supplements their human frailties with cyborg prosthetics that give them an inhuman capacity for human salvation. The cyborg image metaphorically compensates for the modern dissonance between the technological and the organic; it uses technology to weld together the fractured nature of contemporary human beings, creating one inhuman whole that is capable of obtaining a limited perfection precisely because of its inhuman state. Archer achieves this state and triumphs--maybe not an angel, not a "golden one," but certainly a cause for hope.

The emergence of cyborg figures in films is not limited to Face/Off. Over the past two decades, the different facets of the cyborg character have been explored in films as diverse as Blade Runner (1982) and Star Trek: First Contact (1996). These portrayals reflect a deep ambivalence, since many in our culture see the cyborg as a symbol not of hope but of dehumanization, the dead end of the modern world. In Blade Runner, the human hero's job is to hunt down and "cancel" android "replicants" that are "more human than human"; and in First Contact, humans battle to resist "assimilation into the [cy]Borg collective." Steven Spielberg's A.I. (2001) features a twist on the cyborg hero, depicting a robot boy who, like Pinocchio, longs to become "real." In these cases, the films offer positive images of cyborgs as well, suggesting that their future could go either way--or continue to go both ways. Jewel asked the

Palma 20

question: "And where's my hope now that my heroes have gone?" Perhaps the 1991 film <u>Terminator 2: Judgment Day</u> provides the answer, one that speaks to the eventual triumph of the cyborg as hero. Turning to human heroes Sarah and John Connor, the cyborg Terminator says simply, "Come with me if you want to live."

Notes

[1] I want to thank those who have contributed to my thinking on this topic, including my professors and classmates, Professor Morris Beja, and two consultants from the Ohio State University Writing Center, Melissa Goldthwaite and Nels Highberg.

[2] The rewritten version of "Candle in the Wind" that John sang at the funeral of Diana, Princess of Wales, in 1997 is now the best-selling recorded single of all time. Although Diana was not in movies, she was constantly in public view--in newspapers and magazines and on television; she too was caught up in the cult of fame that Monroe experienced. As Diana the person died, Diana the myth was born.

Palma 22

Works Cited

A.I. Dir. Steven Spielberg. Warner Bros., 2001.

Amende, Coral. Hollywood Confidential: An Inside Look at the Public Careers and Private Lives of Hollywood's Rich and Famous. New York: Penguin, 1997.

Beja, Morris. Personal interview. 2 Oct. 2002.

Blade Runner. Dir. Ridley Scott. Warner Bros./Ladd, 1982.

Box Office Bombshell: Marilyn Monroe. Writ. Andy Thomas, Jeff Schefel, and Kevin Burns. Dir. Bill Harris. Narr. Peter Graves. A&E Biography. Arts and Entertainment Network. 23 Oct. 2002.

Corey, Melinda, and George Ochoa. The Dictionary of Film Quotations: 6,000 Provocative Movie Quotes from 1,000 Movies. New York: Crown, 1995.

Daly, Steve. "Face to Face." Entertainment Weekly 20 June 1997: 20-24.

deCordova, Richard. Picture Personalities: The Emergence of the Star System in America. Urbana: U of Illinois P, 1990.

De Meyer, Baron. Mary Pickford, circa 1915. MPTV Images, Los Angeles. 30 Oct. 2002 <http://www.netropolisusa.biz/scripts/CUWP_CGI.EXE>.

Face/Off. Dir. John Woo. Perf. John Travolta and
    Nicolas Cage. Paramount, 1997.
Feeney, F. X. Rev. of The Ref, dir. Ted Demme.
    Mr. Showbiz: A World of Entertainment from
    ABCNEWS.com. 18 Oct. 2002 <http://
    www.mrshowbiz.com/reviews/moviereviews/
    movies/32363.html>.
Gallagher, Brian. "Greta Garbo Is Sad: Some
    Historical Reflections on the Paradoxes of
    Stardom in the American Film Industry, 1910-
    1960." Images: A Journal of Film and Popular
    Culture 3 (1997): 7 pts. 7 Aug. 2002
    <http://www.imagesjournal.com/issue03/
    infocus.htm>.
Gibson, Mel, perf. The Patriot. Dir. Roland
    Emmerich. Sony, 2000.
Haraway, Donna J. "A Cyborg Manifesto: Science,
    Technology, and Socialist-Feminism in the
    Late Twentieth Century." Simians, Cyborgs,
    and Women. New York: Routledge, 1991. 149-
    81.
"Hero." Merriam-Webster's Collegiate Dictionary.
    10th ed. 1996.
John, Elton. "Candle in the Wind." Goodbye Yellow
    Brick Road. MCA, 1973.
Kilcher, Jewel. "Amen." Pieces of You. A&R, 1994.

Palma 24

Little Women. Dir. Gillian Armstrong. Columbia
    Tri-Star, 1994.
Mission: Impossible II. Dir. John Woo. Perf. Tom
    Cruise. Paramount, 2000.
The Princess Bride. Dir. Rob Reiner. 20th
    Century-Fox, 1987.
The Ref. Dir. Ted Demme. Perf. Denis Leary, Judy
    Davis, and Kevin Spacey. Touchstone, 1994.
Rushing, Janice Hocker, and Thomas S. Frentz.
    Projecting the Shadow: The Cyborg Hero in
    American Film. Chicago: U of Chicago P,
    1995.
Smith, Will, perf. Men in Black II. Dir. Barry
    Sonnenfeld. Columbia, 2002.
The Star. Dir. Lawrence Pitkethly. Videocassette.
    CBS/FOX Video, 1995.
A Star Is Born. Dir. George Cukor. Perf. Judy
    Garland. Warner Bros., 1954.
Star Trek: First Contact. Dir. Jonathan Frakes.
    Paramount, 1996.
Star Wars. Dir. George Lucas. 20th Century Fox,
    1977.
Sunset Boulevard. Dir. Billy Wilder. Perf. Gloria
    Swanson. Paramount, 1950.
Terminator 2: Judgment Day. Dir. James Cameron.
    Tri-Star, 1991.

<u>The Three Musketeers</u>. Dir. Stephen Herek. Disney, 1993.

Vaughan, Stephen. <u>Nicolas Cage and John Travolta in</u> Face/Off. 1997. Photofest, New York.

Weaver, Sigourney, perf. <u>Aliens</u>. Dir. James Cameron. 20th Century Fox, 1986.

Chicago Style

The style guide of the University of Chicago Press has long been used in history as well as in other areas of the arts and humanities. The fifteenth edition of *The Chicago Manual of Style,* published in 2003, provides a complete guide to Chicago style. For further reference, you can also consult the following much shorter volume intended for student writers:

```
Turabian, Kate L. A Manual for Writers of Term
     Papers, Theses, and Dissertations. 6th ed.
     Rev. John Grossman and Alice Bennett.
     Chicago: University of Chicago Press, 1996.
```

For easy reference, examples of how to format both Chicago-style notes and bibliographic entries are shown together.

DIRECTORY TO CHICAGO STYLE

In-Text Citations, Notes, and Bibliography
Notes and Bibliographic Entries

BOOKS

1. One author, *148*
2. Multiple authors, *148*
3. Organization as author, *149*
4. Unknown author, *149*
5. Editor, *149*
6. Selection in an anthology or chapter in a book, with an editor, *150*
7. Edition other than the first, *150*
8. Multivolume work, *150*
9. Reference work, *151*

PERIODICALS

10. Article in a journal paginated by volume, *151*
11. Article in a journal paginated by issue, *151*
12. Article in a magazine, *152*
13. Article in a newspaper, *152*

(Continued)

ELECTRONIC SOURCES

14. World Wide Web site, *152*
15. Online book, *153*
16. Article in an electronic journal, *153*
17. Article in an online magazine, *154*
18. Article from a database, *154*
19. Email and other personal communications, *154*

OTHER SOURCES

20. Published or broadcast interview, *155*
21. Video or DVD, *155*
22. CD-ROM, *155*
23. Pamphlet, report, or brochure, *156*
24. Government document, *156*

A Student Research Essay, Chicago Style

Chicago Format for In-Text Citations, Notes, and Bibliography

In Chicago style, you use superscript numbers ([1]) to mark citations in the text. Place the superscript number for each note near the cited material — at the end of the relevant quotation, sentence, clause, or phrase. Type the number after any punctuation mark except the dash; do not leave space between the superscript and the preceding letter or punctuation mark. Number citations sequentially throughout the text.

The notes themselves can be footnotes (each typed at the bottom of the page on which the superscript for it appears in the text) or endnotes (all typed on a separate page at the end of the text under the heading "Notes"). Be sure to check your instructor's preference. The first line of each note is indented like a paragraph (five spaces or one-half inch) and begins with a number followed by a period and one space before the first word of the entry. All remaining lines of the entry are typed flush with the left margin. Footnotes should be single-spaced with a double space between each note. All endnotes should be double-spaced.

IN THE TEXT

Sweig argues that Castro and Che Guevara were not the only key players in the Cuban Revolution of the late 1950s.[19]

IN THE FIRST NOTE

19. Julia Sweig, *Inside the Cuban Revolution* (Cambridge, MA: Harvard University Press, 2002), 9.

After giving complete information the first time you cite a work, shorten any additional references to that work: list only the author's name followed by a comma, a shortened version of the title, a comma, and the page number. If the reference is to the same source cited in the previous note, you can use the Latin abbreviation *Ibid.* (for "in the same place") instead of the name and title.

IN SUBSEQUENT NOTES

19. Julia Sweig, *Inside the Cuban Revolution* (Cambridge, MA: Harvard University Press, 2002), 9.

20. Ibid., 13.

21. Foner and Lewis, *Black Worker*, 138-39.

22. Ferguson, "Comfort of Being Sad," 63.

23. Sweig, *Cuban Revolution*, 21.

An alphabetical list of the sources you use in your paper is usually titled *Bibliography* in Chicago style. If "Sources Consulted," "Works Cited," or "Selected Bibliography" better describes your list, however, any of these titles is acceptable.

In the bibliographic entry for a source, include the same information as in the first note for that source, but omit the specific page reference. However, give the *first* author's last name first, followed by a comma and the first name; separate the main elements of the entry with periods rather than commas; and do not enclose the publication information for books in parentheses.

IN THE BIBLIOGRAPHY

```
Sweig, Julia. Inside the Cuban Revolution.
    Cambridge, MA: Harvard University Press,
    2002.
```

Start the bibliography on a separate page after the main text and any endnotes. Continue the consecutive numbering of pages. Type the title "Bibliography" (without italics or quotation marks) and center it one inch below the top of the page. Begin each entry at the left margin. Indent the second and subsequent lines of each entry five spaces (or one-half inch). Double-space the entire list.

List sources alphabetically by authors' last names (or by the first major word in the title if the author is unknown). If you use software (Microsoft Word, EndNote, Research Assistant) to collect and format your bibliography, remember to double-check that all formatting is correct.

Chicago Format for Notes and Bibliographic Entries

For easy reference, the following examples demonstrate how to format both notes and bibliographic entries according to Chicago style.

Books

1. ONE AUTHOR

1. James S. Hirsch, *Riot and Remembrance: The Tulsa Race War and Its Legacy* (Boston: Houghton Mifflin, 2002), 119.

Hirsch, James S. *Riot and Remembrance: The Tulsa Race War and Its Legacy.* Boston: Houghton Mifflin, 2002.

2. MULTIPLE AUTHORS

2. Margaret Macmillan and Richard Holbrooke, *Paris 1919: Six Months That Changed the World* (New York: Random House, 2003), 384.

Macmillan, Margaret, and Richard Holbrooke. *Paris 1919: Six Months That Changed the World.* New York: Random House, 2003.

When there are more than three authors, it is acceptable in Chicago style to give the first-listed author followed by *et al.* or *and others* in the note. In the bibliography, however, list all the authors' names.

2. Stephen J. Blank and others, *Conflict, Culture, and History: Regional Dimensions* (Miami: University Press of the Pacific, 2002), 276.

Blank, Stephen J., Lawrence E. Grinter, Karl P. Magyar, Lewis B. Ware, and Bynum E. Weathers. *Conflict, Culture, and History:*

Regional Dimensions. Miami: University Press of the Pacific, 2002.

3. ORGANIZATION AS AUTHOR

3. World Intellectual Property Organization, *Intellectual Property Profile of the Least Developed Countries* (Geneva: World Intellectual Property Organization, 2002), 43.

World Intellectual Property Organization. *Intellectual Property Profile of the Least Developed Countries*. Geneva: World Intellectual Property Organization, 2002.

4. UNKNOWN AUTHOR

4. *Broad Stripes and Bright Stars* (Kansas City, MO: Andrews McMeel Publishing, 2002), 10.

Broad Stripes and Bright Stars. Kansas City, MO: Andrews McMeel Publishing, 2002.

5. EDITOR

5. James H. Fetzer, ed., *The Great Zapruder Film Hoax: Deceit and Deception in the Death of JFK* (Chicago: Open Court Publishing, 2003), 56.

Fetzer, James H., ed. *The Great Zapruder Film Hoax: Deceit and Deception in the Death of JFK.* Chicago: Open Court Publishing, 2003.

6. SELECTION IN AN ANTHOLOGY OR CHAPTER IN A BOOK, WITH AN EDITOR

6. Denise Little, "Born in Blood," in *Alternate Gettysburgs*, ed. Brian Thomsen and Martin H. Greenberg (New York: Berkley Publishing Group, 2002), 245.

Little, Denise. "Born in Blood." *In Alternate Gettysburgs*, edited by Brian Thomsen and Martin H. Greenberg, 242-55. New York: Berkley Publishing Group, 2002.

7. EDITION OTHER THAN THE FIRST

7. Charles G. Beaudette, *Excess Heat: Why Cold Fusion Research Prevailed*, 2nd ed. (South Bristol, ME: Oak Grove Press, 2002), 313.

Beaudette, Charles G. *Excess Heat: Why Cold Fusion Research Prevailed.* 2nd ed. South Bristol, ME: Oak Grove Press, 2002.

8. MULTIVOLUME WORK

8. John Watson, *Annals of Philadelphia and Pennsylvania in the Olden Time*, vol. 2 (Washington, DC: Ross & Perry, 2003), 514.

Watson, John. *Annals of Philadelphia and Pennsylvania in the Olden Time.* Vol. 2. Washington, DC: Ross & Perry, 2003.

9. REFERENCE WORK

Cite well-known reference works in your notes, but do not list them in your bibliography. Use *s.v.,* the abbreviation for the Latin *sub verbo* ("under the word") to let your reader know what you looked up in the reference work.

```
9. Encarta World Dictionary, s.v.
"carpetbagger."
```

Periodicals

10. ARTICLE IN A JOURNAL PAGINATED BY VOLUME

When a journal's issues are numbered, place a comma after the volume number, insert the abbreviation *no.* and the issue number.

```
10. Diane Kirkby, "'Beer, Glorious Beer':
Gender Politics and Australian Popular Culture,"
Journal of Popular Culture 37, no. 2 (2003): 246.

Kirkby, Diane. "'Beer, Glorious Beer': Gender
     Politics and Australian Popular Culture."
     Journal of Popular Culture 37, no. 2 (2003):
     244-56.
```

11. ARTICLE IN A JOURNAL PAGINATED BY ISSUE

```
11. Karin Lützen, "The Female World: Viewed
from Denmark," Journal of Women's History 12, no.
3 (2000): 36.

Lützen, Karin. "The Female World: Viewed from
     Denmark." Journal of Women's History 12, no.
     3 (2000): 34-38.
```

12. ARTICLE IN A MAGAZINE

12. Douglas Brinkley and Anne Brinkley, "Lawyers and Lizard-Heads," *Atlantic Monthly,* May 2002, 56.

Brinkley, Douglas, and Anne Brinkley. "Lawyers and Lizard-Heads." *Atlantic Monthly,* May 2002, 55-61.

13. ARTICLE IN A NEWSPAPER

13. Caroline E. Mayer, "Wireless Industry to Adopt Voluntary Standards," *Washington Post,* September 9, 2003, sec. E.

Mayer, Caroline E. "Wireless Industry to Adopt Voluntary Standards." Washington Post, September 9, 2003, sec. E.

Electronic Sources

14. WORLD WIDE WEB SITE

14. Rutgers University, "Picture Gallery," *The Rutgers Oral History Archives of World War II,* http://fas-history.rutgers.edu/oralhistory/orlhom.htm (accessed November 7, 2003).

Rutgers University. "Picture Gallery." *The Rutgers Oral History Archives of World War II.* http://fas-history.rutgers.edu/

oralhistory/orlhom.htm (accessed November 7, 2003).

15. ONLINE BOOK

15. Janja Bec, *The Shattering of the Soul* (Los Angeles: The Simon Wiesenthal Center, 1997), http://motlc.wiesenthal.com/resources/books/shatteringsoul/index.html (accessed November 6, 2003).

Bec, Janja. *The Shattering of the Soul.* Los Angeles: The Simon Wiesenthal Center, 1997. http://motlc.wiesenthal.com/resources/books/shatteringsoul/index.html (accessed November 6, 2003).

16. ARTICLE IN AN ELECTRONIC JOURNAL

Always include the page numbers, if available, when you are citing articles in journals that also have print versions.

16. Damian Bracken, "Rationalism and the Bible in Seventh-Century Ireland," *Chronicon 2* (1998), http://www.ucc.ie/chronicon/bracfra.htm (accessed November 1, 2003).

Bracken, Damian. "Rationalism and the Bible in Seventh-Century Ireland." *Chronicon 2* (1998). http://www.ucc.ie/chronicon/bracfra.htm (accessed November 1, 2003).

17. ARTICLE IN AN ONLINE MAGAZINE

```
    17. Kim Iskyan, "Putin's Next Power Play,"
Slate, November 4, 2003, http://slate.msn.com/id/
2090745 (accessed November 7, 2003).
```

```
Iskyan, Kim. "Putin's Next Power Play." Slate,
    November 4, 2003. http://slate.msn.com/id/
    2090745 (accessed November 7, 2003).
```

18. ARTICLE FROM A DATABASE

```
    18. Peter DeMarco, "Holocaust Survivors
Lend Voice to History," Boston Globe, November 2,
2003, http://www.lexis-nexis.com (accessed
November 19, 2003).
```

```
DeMarco, Peter. "Holocaust Survivors Lend Voice
    to History." Boston Globe, November 2, 2003.
    http://www.lexis-nexis.com (accessed
    November 19, 2003).
```

19. EMAIL AND OTHER PERSONAL COMMUNICATIONS

Cite email messages and other personal communications, such as letters and telephone calls, in the text or in a note. Do not cite personal communications in your bibliography.

```
    19. Kareem Adas, email message to author,
February 11, 2004.
```

Other Sources

20. PUBLISHED OR BROADCAST INTERVIEW

20. Condoleezza Rice, interview by Charlie Rose, *The Charlie Rose Show,* PBS, October 30, 2003.

Rice, Condoleezza. Interview by Charlie Rose. *The Charlie Rose Show.* PBS, October 30, 2003.

Interviews you conduct are considered personal communications.

21. VIDEO OR DVD

21. Edward Norton and Edward Furlong, *American History X,* DVD, directed by Tony Kaye (1998; Los Angeles: New Line Studios, 2002).

Norton, Edward, and Edward Furlong. *American History X.* DVD. Directed by Tony Kaye. 1998. Los Angeles: New Line Studios, 2002.

22. CD-ROM

22. *The Civil War,* CD-ROM (Fogware Publishing, 2000).

The Civil War. CD-ROM. Fogware Publishing, 2000.

23. PAMPHLET, REPORT, OR BROCHURE

Information about the author or publisher may not be readily available, but give enough information to identify your source.

23. Jamie McCarthy, *Who Is David Irving?* (San Antonio, TX: The Holocaust History Project, 1998).

McCarthy, Jamie. *Who Is David Irving?* San
 Antonio, TX: The Holocaust History Project,
 1998.

24. GOVERNMENT DOCUMENT

24. House Committee on Ways and Means, *Report on Trade Mission to Sub-Saharan Africa,* 108th Cong., 1st sess. (Washington, DC: U.S. Government Printing Office, 2003), 28.

House Committee on Ways and Means. *Report on
 Trade Mission to Sub-Saharan Africa.* 108th
 Cong., 1st sess. Washington, DC: U.S.
 Government Printing Office, 2003.

A Student Research Essay, Chicago Style

An introductory history course on U.S. civilization to 1877 called on students to write an essay "of no more than six pages focusing on a controversial issue related to the First Amendment. Be sure to summarize historical events, analyze the significance of the issue, and use appropriate source material from class readings or additional research you do on your own."

Kelly Darr chose to review the 1803 *Marbury v. Madison* decision and to relate that decision to the growth of the Supreme Court's powers. As is often appropriate in humanities essays, the opening paragraph introduces the subject and concludes with an explicit thesis, this one in the form of two major questions that serve as an organizational guide to the remainder of the essay and as a promise to the reader of what is to come. The middle paragraphs provide textual evidence in response to the first question, while the concluding paragraphs address the second question and consider the status of this decision today.

Marbury v. Madison
and the Origins of Judicial Review

Kelly Darr

History 17A
Professor O'Brien
March 3, 2003

The Supreme Court of the United States is a very prestigious and powerful branch of American government today. Perhaps the most notable demonstration of the Court's power was its decision concerning the presidential election of 2000, a decision that resulted in George W. Bush becoming president.[1] The Court has not always held this position, however. When the government system was developed in the late eighteenth century, the powers of the judicial branch were fairly undefined. In 1803, Chief Justice John Marshall, with his decision in *Marbury v. Madison*, began to define the duties of the Court by claiming for the Supreme Court the power of judicial review. Judicial review has been upheld ever since, and many people take the practice for granted. There is controversy around Marshall's decision, however, with some claiming that judicial review was not the intent of the Framers. Two questions must be asked: Did Marshall overstep his bounds when he declared judicial review for the Court? If so, why has his decision been upheld for two hundred years? An examination of the actual case, *Marbury v. Madison*, and of Marshall's reasons for his decision is the first step to answering these questions.

Darr 3

This case was surrounded by personal and political opposition. It was brought to the Court by William Marbury, whose commission as justice of the peace by John Adams was withheld by Thomas Jefferson when he became president. Jefferson's act was prompted by Adams's attempt to fill the national judiciary with Federalist judges on the eve before Jefferson took office. Due to a mistake by John Marshall himself (at the time, the secretary of state under Adams), however, the commissions were not delivered. Jefferson, who did not appreciate the last-minute attempt to fill the offices with Federalists, refused to deliver the commissions after he took office. Marbury and a few other men sued James Madison, secretary of state under Jefferson. Marshall, now the chief justice, was eager to try the case and attack Jefferson, his political enemy.[2]

By the time the case went to trial in 1803, two of the five years of the term for justice of the peace had expired. It was no longer a case over undelivered commissions; it was a case testing the power of the courts against the executive. The attorney for Marbury, Charles Lee, proved through several witnesses that the commissions had been signed and sealed by Adams, so Jefferson therefore had to turn them over to the appointees. After Lee's summation, the defense presented no case; the attorney general announced that he had not been instructed to appear. Jefferson had control politically of the Congress, so he just sat back and waited for his adversary's decision. If Marshall issued a writ of mandamus requiring Madison to hand over the commissions, Jefferson could have him impeached.[3] If Marshall ruled in favor of Jefferson, he would make the judicial branch look even more powerless than it already did. Marshall was in a no-win situation, and he was aware of this predicament when he set out to make his decision.[4]

He finally made his decision on February 24, 1803, and it was based on two concerns: the ethics of withholding Marbury's commission, and the right of the Supreme Court to issue a writ of mandamus to the president.[5] Marshall broke the issue into three questions. The first question addressed whether Marbury had a right to the commission. Marshall said that he did have the right to it because it had been signed by the president at the time and sealed with the seal of the United States. Second, Marshall asked, if Marbury did have a right to the commission, whether the laws of the land protected his right to the appointment. Marshall reasoned that withholding his commission would be in violation of his personal rights, so the laws must protect

Darr 5

those rights. Third, Marshall asked if the laws protected Marbury in the form of a writ of mandamus from the Supreme Court. Marshall reasoned that the Court could not issue a writ of mandamus even though the Judiciary Act of 1789 said that it could. According to this law, the Supreme Court could issue writs of mandamus to people under the authority of the United States, which Marbury clearly was; however, if the Court could not issue a writ of mandamus, then this law was unconstitutional. He went on to say that the Supreme Court had only appellate jurisdiction (except in a few specific cases) and this case had been brought before the Court for original jurisdiction. Therefore, he declared that the law stating that the Supreme Court could issue writs of mandamus was unconstitutional. In other words, Congress did not have the legal power to give the Court that right. He went on to say that the Constitution was the supreme law of the land, and since it was the judicial branch's duty to say what the law was, they had the power to declare acts unconstitutional. Thus Marshall denied mandamus for Marbury and ruled in favor of Madison. At the same time, however, he took a big step toward strengthening the judicial branch by establishing the power of judicial review.[6]

Marshall's reasons for his decision were shaky and have been the source of controversy ever since. Even though his decision was legally weak, it was politically ingenious. He ruled in favor of his opponent, Jefferson, but at the same time increased the power of the judicial branch. He also did not order a writ of mandamus to Jefferson, therefore eliminating the possibility of impeachment.[7]

In addition, Marshall did not order anyone to do or refrain from doing anything that they could refuse to do and thus repudiate his decision. Jefferson and the Antifederalist party could not do the opposite of what Marshall ordered to oppose his ruling because Marshall did not order Jefferson to do anything. Chief Justice Marshall gained independence and importance for the Supreme Court, as well as gaining a personal victory against Jefferson and his administration.[8]

The power of judicial review has been reserved for the Supreme Court since *Marbury v. Madison*, but some feel that it is not a constitutional precedent. They maintain that Marshall used weak arguments to claim the power of review when it was not intended by the Framers to be exclusive to the judicial branch. These people

Darr 7

find many faults with Marshall's arguments. First of all, Marshall reasoned that the justices have to take an oath to support and defend the Constitution and therefore they should have the power to decide which laws agree with the Constitution. His critics claim that this line of reasoning is flawed because this type of oath is taken by every government official. Because the oath only applies to the duties of the job, it does not give the Court judicial review, and Marshall gave no other reasons than this oath.[9] Others state that the power of review was intended by the Framers for the executive and legislative branches as well, and that the other two branches still possess this power, but we have been wrongly following the precedent of *Marbury v. Madison* since 1803. They feel that the executive and legislative branches could use this power as well against the Court. Because the Supreme Court is aware of that, the Court declares acts unconstitutional more frequently on the state and local levels than on the federal level. The power of judicial review violates the separation of powers and has led to judicial supremacy, according to these historians.[10] A third fault attributed to Marshall is that, since he was the secretary of state under Adams and directly involved in the situation that brought about this case, he should not have presided over the hearing.[11]

Many presidents and politicians, such as Benjamin Franklin, Abraham Lincoln, and Andrew Jackson, have disagreed with the power of judicial review. Despite the controversy, it is still upheld today.[12] It seems logical that it has survived because it obviously works. Some branch of government needs to be able to declare acts unconstitutional; it is essential to the system of checks and balances. If this power were shared between the branches, then a decision would become a question of what political party had the most weight in each branch at that moment. If one party had the majority in the executive branch and in the Congress, then it could declare the Court unconstitutional or ignore the Court's rulings. The ruling most likely has been upheld because the power of review must be practiced in order for the Constitution to be the supreme law of the land. Since the Constitution does not definitely assign this power to one branch, it works best if one branch has the power in order to give review any weight at all. The other branches may be aware of this but just wish the power belonged to their branch.

Notes

1. *Bush v. Gore*, 531 U.S. 98 (2000), http://supct.law.cornell.edu/supct/html/00-949.ZPC.html (accessed February 8, 2003).

2. John A. Garraty, *Quarrels That Have Shaped the Constitution* (New York: Harper and Row, 1987), 7-14.

3. Ibid., 19.

4. William C. Louthan, *The United States Supreme Court: Lawmaking in the Third Branch of Government* (Englewood Cliffs, NJ: Prentice-Hall, 1991), 51.

5. Thomas J. Higgins, *Judicial Review Unmasked* (West Hanover, MA: Christopher Publishing House, 1981), 40-41.

6. *Marbury v. Madison*, 5 U.S. 137 (1803).

7. Louthan, *Supreme Court*, 51.

8. Ibid.

9. Ibid., 50-51.

10. Higgins, *Judicial Review*, 40-41.

11. Ibid., 32.

12. Ibid., 34.

Bibliography

Bush v. Gore. 531 U.S. 98 (2000). http://supct.law.cornell.edu/supct/html/00-949.ZPC.html (accessed February 8, 2003).

Garraty, John A. *Quarrels That Have Shaped the Constitution*. New York: Harper and Row, 1987.

Higgins, Thomas J. *Judicial Review Unmasked*. West Hanover, MA: Christopher Publishing House, 1981.

Louthan, William C. *The United States Supreme Court: Lawmaking in the Third Branch of Government*. Englewood Cliffs, NJ: Prentice-Hall, 1991.

Marbury v. Madison. 5 U.S. 137 (1803).

6

Research in the Social Sciences

Resources in the Social Sciences

GENERAL REFERENCE SOURCES FOR THE SOCIAL SCIENCES

International Encyclopedia of the Social and Behavioral Sciences. 24 vols. plus 2 index vols. 2001. Supplies 4,000 articles about topics and terms from the major areas in the social and behavioral sciences. (online by subscription)

INDEXES AND DATABASES FOR THE SOCIAL SCIENCES

ABI/INFORM OnDisc. 1971–. Indexes and abstracts academic and popular periodicals. (online by subscription, CD-ROM)

PAIS International in Print. 1991–. Formerly *PAIS Bulletin*, 1976–90; *PAIS Foreign Language Index*, 1972–90; and *Public Affairs Information Service Bulletin*, 1915–76. Indexes over twelve hundred social science periodicals plus pamphlets, agency reports, government documents, and books on politics, economics, business administration, international relations, and social topics. (online by subscription, CD-ROM)

Social Science Source. 1984–. Indexes over three hundred periodicals and supplies full text of articles from fifteen publications emphasizing current trends in the social and political sciences. (CD-ROM)

Social Sciences Citation Index. 1956–. Indexes citations made in over a thousand social science journals; entries allow tracing influence through the frequency of later citations of books and periodicals. (online by subscription, CD-ROM)

Social Sciences Index. 1974–. Formerly *Social Sciences and Humanities Index*, 1965–74, and *International Index*, 1907–65. Indexes and abstracts (on CD-ROM) articles from over three hundred major periodicals on policy sciences, psychology, sociology, social work, gerontology, health, law, criminology, law enforcement, public administration, urban studies, political science, international relations, geography, and many other social science areas. (online by subscription, CD-ROM)

WEB RESOURCES FOR THE SOCIAL SCIENCES

Fedstats: One Stop Shopping for Federal Statistics
<http://www.fedstats.gov>
Consolidates access to statistics and data from over seventy federal agencies.

Infomine: Scholarly Internet Resource Collections
<http://infomine.ucr.edu>
Supplies indexed and annotated links to databases, government resources, maps, teaching resources, and other materials of academic interest for business, law, geography, and other social sciences.

Quick Reference
<http://www.lib.utexas.edu/Libs/PCL/Reference.html>
Provides access to business and reference resources.

Social Science Data and Databases
<http://www.tntech.edu/www/acad/hist/data.html>
Provides links to general social science Web sites.

SOSIG: Social Science Information Gateway
<http://sosig.esrc.bris.ac.uk>
Facilitates access to thousands of selected resources organized by subject areas or geography.

U.S. Census Bureau Home Page
<http://www.census.gov>
Supplies demographic, economic, and social data about the U.S. population.

Voice of the Shuttle: Web Page for Humanities Research
  <http://vos.ucsb.edu>
  Specializes in highlights, top sites, and links to extensive resources in the humanities but also includes anthropology, archaeology, business, law, and political science as well as regional, cultural, media, minority, and gender studies.

The Webliography: Internet Subject Guides
  <http://www.jsr.cc.va.us/lrc/guides.htm>
  Provides extensive annotated guides to Web resources in the social sciences, including business, economics, ethnic studies, psychology, social work, women's studies, and many others.

Anthropology

GENERAL REFERENCE SOURCES FOR ANTHROPOLOGY

Encyclopedia of Anthropology. 1976. Supplies articles, many illustrated, defining and explaining anthropological terms and topics and including biographical entries.

INDEXES AND DATABASES FOR ANTHROPOLOGY

Abstracts in Anthropology. 1970–. Indexes and abstracts articles from periodicals about physical, linguistic, and cultural anthropology and about archeological sites and artifacts.

Anthropological Literature. 1979–. Indexes articles and essays on anthropology and archaeology, including art history, demography, economics, and religious studies. (online by subscription)

WEB RESOURCES FOR ANTHROPOLOGY

Anthro.net
  <http://anthro.net/>
  Allows searches and provides extensive links to reviewed sites and bibliographic references in anthropology and archaeology.

Anthropology in the News
  <http://www.tamu.edu/anthropology/news.html>
  Lists links to current anthropology-related news stories.

Anthropology Resources on the Internet
  <http://www.aaanet.org/resinet.htm>
  Links to an extensive array of resources on anthropology and archaeology, also including academic institutions, museums, and electronic discussion groups.

Anthro TECH: Central On-Line Clearing House for Anthropological Resources & Web Services
  <http://www.anthrotech.com>
  Supplies images and links to resources in applied, cultural, linguistic, and physical anthropology as well as archaeology.

ArchNet
  <http://archnet.asu.edu>
  Links to resources and field sites in archaeology, grouped by region, subject, museum, academic institution, and so forth.

Fieldwork: The Anthropologist in the Field
  <http://www.truman.edu/academics/ss/faculty/tamakoshil/intro.html>
  Creates a "fieldwork experience" including definitions of terms, graphics, and information about the procedures of anthropologists in the field.

UCSB Department of Anthropology Links Directory
  <http://www.anth.ucsb.edu/links/pages>
  Provides links to various anthropological topics, journals, and organizations.

The WWW Virtual Library: Anthropology
  <http://vlib.anthrotech.com/>
  Allows keyword searches and provides annotated links to many subfields of anthropology.

Business and Economics

GENERAL REFERENCE SOURCES FOR BUSINESS AND ECONOMICS

Encyclopedia of Banking and Finance. 1991. Includes brief definitions of terms and longer explanations of trends, historical background, government regulations, and related topics.

International Encyclopedia of Business and Management. 6 vols. 2002. Includes 500 entries covering biographies of important figures and general and country-specific business and management topics.

International Encyclopedia of Economics. 1997. Contains almost 400 articles that cover topics ranging from monetary theory and international trade to welfare economics and the history of economic thought.

McGraw-Hill Dictionary of Modern Economics. 1994. Defines key terms and supplies bibliographies, tables, and graphs.

The New Palgrave: A Dictionary of Economics. 1987. Supplies thousands of entries, including bibliographies on economic history, methods, philosophy, theories, controversies, and major figures.

Occupational Outlook Handbook. 1949–. Biennial. Offers information about more than two hundred occupations, including requirements, conditions, earnings, locations, and projections. (online at <http://www.bls.gov/oco./>, CD-ROM)

INDEXES AND DATABASES FOR BUSINESS AND ECONOMICS

Business Index. 1979–. Covers last four years, and indexes more than eight hundred business periodicals and newspapers as well as hundreds of other sources. (online by subscription, CD-ROM, and microfilm versions)

Business Periodicals Index. 1958–. Formerly *Industrial Arts Index*, 1913–57. Indexes and abstracts articles from over 250 business periodicals and newspapers. (online by subscription, CD-ROM as *Wilson Business Abstracts*)

Encyclopedia of Business Information Sources. 1988. Lists indexes of periodicals, databases, sources of statistical information, organizations, and other resources available on hundreds of business topics.

International Bibliography of Economics. 1955–. Lists articles, books, and other resources about economics, including history and policy, as well as topics such as money, income, production, and markets.

Predicasts F&S Index: United States. 1972–. Indexes by industry, product, and company name, supplying full text and abstracts from over 750 periodicals on business and financial topics. (online by subscription, CD-ROM)

WEB RESOURCES FOR BUSINESS AND ECONOMICS

The BizTech Network
   <http://www.brint.com/>
   Allows searches and provides links to articles, papers, magazines, tools, and many other resources for "contemporary business, management, and information technology issues."

Business and Economics Resources
   <http://www.ipl.org/div/subject/browse/bus00.00.00/>
   Alphabetically lists links to many different resources, including sites on careers in the business world.

Business Week Online
   <http://www.businessweek.com/>
   Offers online versions of some *BW* stories, quick news updates, stock and mutual-fund tracking data, and advertisements—some of which may, in fact, be useful.

Economics Working Paper Archive
   <http://econwpa.wustl.edu>
   Includes working papers in economics, organized by subject areas, with many links to other sites and sources.

Galaxy Business General Resources
   <http://www.einet.net/galaxy/Business-and-Commerce
   /Business-General-Resources.html>
   Links to a variety of resources for business; includes prices, statistics, trends, and general reading sources.

International Business Resources on the WWW
   <http://ciber.bus.msu.edu>
   Specializes in links to international business sites. Also offers keyword searches, browsing, and a variety of other links.

Internet and Marketing
   <http://www.ntu.edu.sg/library/mktg/int-mktg.htm>
   A site geared to advertising and marketing on the Internet; offers links to statistics, market research, and other resources.

The Management Archive
   <http://ursus.jun.alaska.edu/>
   Provides information on managing business and public organizations, with links to an archive of working papers, other management sites, and a search facility.

Rutgers Accounting Web
   <http://accounting.rutgers.edu/>
   Contains information and links to all areas of accounting, including searches and resources on finance, taxation, government agencies, and publications.

SEC EDGAR Database
   <http://www.sec.gov/edgar.shtml>
   The Electronic Data Gathering, Analysis, and Retrieval system is the Securities and Exchange Commission's archive of business filings. Includes various search capabilities and a wide range of information.

WebEc
   <http://www.helsinki.fi/WebEc/WebEc.html>
   An award-winning site that attempts to categorize all the free information on economics available on the Web. Organized by area of economics, it is easily searchable and includes the valuable List of Economics Journals.

Communications, Journalism, and Linguistics

GENERAL REFERENCE SOURCES FOR COMMUNICATIONS, JOURNALISM, AND LINGUISTICS

Communication Yearbook. 1977–. Includes essays reviewing current topics each year from various viewpoints.

Encyclopedic Dictionary of Semiotics, Media, and Communications. 2000. Includes entries that define and describe terms, concepts, people, schools of thought, and movements in various disciplines, including semiotics, media and communication studies, anthropology, psychology, and computer science.

International Encyclopedia of Communications. 4 vols. 1989. Supplies extended entries on communications—ancient and modern, verbal and nonverbal—as well as historical and current influences and processes.

International Encyclopedia of Linguistics. 4 vols. 1991. Provides entries, generally with bibliographies, on linguistic terms and topics, languages, language families, and related topics.

Webster's New World Dictionary of Media and Communications. 1990. Supplies brief entries defining terms used in publishing, broadcasting, journalism, film, public relations, and related areas.

INDEXES AND DATABASES FOR COMMUNICATIONS, JOURNALISM, AND LINGUISTICS

Communication Abstracts. 1978–. Indexes and abstracts articles from communication and speech periodicals. (online by subscription)

Language and Language Behavior Abstracts: LLBA. 1967–. Provides the definitive index to materials on the nature and use of language. Covers research in linguistics (the nature and structure of human speech), in language (speech sounds, sentence and word structure, meaning in language forms, spelling, phonetics), and in pathologies of speech, language, and hearing. (online by subscription, CD-ROM)

WEB RESOURCES FOR COMMUNICATIONS, JOURNALISM, AND LINGUISTICS

American Amateur Press Association
<http://members.aol.com/aapa96>
Provides examples of amateur journalism, tips from professional journalists, and links to resources for writers.

American Communication Association Homepage
<http://www.americancomm.org>
The American Communication Association sponsors this full-coverage page, with links to the different subfields that make up communications, organized by field and by interest.

APDA
<http://www.mit.edu/activities/debate/tournaments.html>
The American Parliamentary Debate Association maintains this site for college and university debating, with links to members, officers, a newsletter, and other debating sites.

CMU Rhetoric and Composition
<http://english-www.hss.cmu.edu/rhetoric/>
A well-organized list of links to classical rhetoric, e-journals, writing centers, rhetoricians, and miscellaneous resources on the Net. An especially good collection of classical texts.

Communication Studies
   <http://www.lib.uiowa.edu/gw/comm/>
   From the University of Iowa; offers a wide range of links to listservs, journals, Web research, and electronic style guides, as well as to a broad range of fields from advertising through rhetoric.

Investigative Reporters & Editors
   <http://www.ire.org>
   An organization dedicated to teaching the skills and issues of investigative journalism; the site's resource center includes a database of more than eleven thousand abstracts of investigative articles.

Linguistic Society of America
   <http://www.lsadc.org>
   Provides information on many aspects of linguistics and links to other resources.

Links to Friendly Communications Homepages
   <http://www.csufresno.edu/speechcomm/wscalink.htm>
   From the Western States Speech Association; provides easy access to many organizational homepages in communications.

News on the Net
   <http://www.reporter.org/news>
   Provides links to numerous news sources, including newspapers, magazines, and TV stations.

SIL International
   <http://www.sil.org>
   Offers information about language communities worldwide. Supports research in all areas of linguistics.

The WWW Virtual Library: Journalism
   <http://209.8.151.142/vlj.html>
   Provides search capability and numerous links to resources on media, broadcasting, communications, and news.

Education

GENERAL REFERENCE SOURCES FOR EDUCATION

Encyclopedia of Education. 10 vols. 1971. Supplies full articles, especially on historical topics.

Encyclopedia of Educational Research. 4 vols. 1992. Summarizes research studies and includes bibliographies.

Encyclopedia of Physical Education, Fitness, and Sports. 4 vols. 1991. Includes articles on historical topics, fitness, training, nutrition, exercise, and specific activities and sports.

The International Encyclopedia of Education. 12 vols. 1994. Contains over 1,200 entries organized alphabetically within 22 major categories, including adult education, girls and women in education, policy and planning, and vocational education and training.

International Encyclopedia of Education: Research and Studies. 10 vols. 1992. Supplies full entries on many general and specialized areas of education.

INDEXES AND DATABASES FOR EDUCATION

Current Index to Journals in Education (CIJE). 1969-. Indexes and abstracts articles from education periodicals; *Resources in Education* (1966-) abstracts unpublished materials such as reports and curriculum guides. (online by subscription, CD-ROM in ERIC)

Education: A Guide to Reference and Information Sources. 1989. Guide to books, periodicals, and databases about education.

Education Index. 1929-. Indexes articles from over 350 education periodicals. (online by subscription, CD-ROM)

ERIC (Educational Resources Information Center). 1966-. Lists more than 750,000 articles, papers, and reports on education. (online by subscription, CD-ROM)

Physical Education Index. 1978-. Indexes articles on physical education and sports from several hundred periodicals.

WEB RESOURCES FOR EDUCATION

AskERIC: Education Information with the Personal Touch
<http://ericir.syr.edu>
Provides access to the ERIC database, current research information, and education news, as well as links through its question-and-answer feature to an array of education, government, and library sites.

EdWeb: Exploring Technology and School Reform
<http://edwebproject.org/wwwedu.html>
Supplies lively information and access to resources on education, educational policy, current reform efforts, and the impact of technological innovation on education.

National Center for Education Statistics (NCES)
<http://nces.ed.gov/>
Provides access to information about U.S. education, including publications, surveys, and other data on student achievement, current issues, and specific topics.

The National Library of Education
<http://www.ed.gov/NLE>
Supplies links to libraries, including federal libraries, and other educational resources.

U.S. Department of Education (ED)
<http://www.ed.gov/>
Includes information on federal education priorities, financial aid, federal programs and funding, publications, research, statistics, and brief ERIC Digests on timely topics (prepared by the various ERIC Clearinghouses around the country).

Ethnic Studies

GENERAL REFERENCE SOURCES FOR ETHNIC STUDIES

The American Indian: A Multimedia Encyclopedia. 1993. Supplies history, tribal backgrounds, documents, songs, biographies, maps, and other information about Native Americans. (CD-ROM)

Asian American Almanac. 1996. Explores the culture and history of American descendents of Asian and Pacific Island immigrants.

The Asian American Encyclopedia. 1995. Discusses the history, language, and culture of both large and small groups of Asian Americans—Chinese, Filipinos, Japanese, Indians, Koreans, Vietnamese, Hmong, and Pacific Islanders—and their influences on and experiences in American culture.

Atlas of the North American Indian. 1985. Includes maps, illustrations, and explanatory text on Native American history, culture, migrations, lands, wars, and other topics from ancient to recent times.

Blackwell Companion to Jewish Culture: From the Eighteenth Century to the Present. 1989. Supplies articles on Jewish culture, notable figures, and contributions in the humanities, sciences, and social sciences.

Dictionary of Asian American History. 1986. Provides essays and brief definitions on the history of Asians and Pacific Islanders in the United States, including cultural and social background, major events, and legal history.

Dictionary of Mexican American History. 1981. Includes entries on history, politics, and social topics including a chronology, a glossary, statistical tables, and maps.

Encyclopedia of Native American Tribes. 1988. Supplies articles, including illustrations, about 150 tribes and general topics.

Encyclopedia of World Cultures. 10 vols. 1991. Supplies entries and bibliographies on all cultural groups.

Handbook of North American Indians. 20 vols. 1988. Provides essays, including bibliographies and illustrations, on many cultural and historical topics.

Harvard Encyclopedia of American Ethnic Groups. 1980–. Contains articles, maps, and tables on 106 ethnic groups, regional groups, and related topics.

The Hispanic-American Almanac. 1993. Discusses Hispanic American history and present-day issues, and includes bibliographies, illustrations, lists, and other materials.

A Native American Encyclopedia: History, Culture, and Peoples. 2000. Provides information on contemporary and historical customs, dress, habitat, weapons, government, and religions of over 200 North American Indian groups; organized by geographical area and alphabetically within each area.

The Negro Almanac: A Reference Work on the African American. 1990. Discusses African American history and present-day issues, and includes a bibliography, illustrations, lists, and other data.

Sourcebook of Hispanic Culture in the United States. 1982. Supplies annotated entries on books, periodicals, and other materials about major Hispanic groups.

The State of Black America. 1976–. Includes articles on various social, economic, political, legal, and educational topics of current concern, analyzed by the National Urban League.

We the People: An Atlas of America's Ethnic Diversity. 1988. Supplies maps, explanatory text, and bibliographies on the origins and migrations of sixty-six ethnic groups.

INDEXES AND DATABASES FOR ETHNIC STUDIES

Afro-American Reference: An Annotated Bibliography of Selected Sources. 1985. Supplies annotated entries about reference books and research collections on African Americans.

Asian American Studies: An Annotated Bibliography and Research Guide. 1989. Lists books and articles on a range of topics.

Chicano Index. 1989–. Formerly *Chicano Periodical Index,* 1967–88. Indexes resources on Mexican Americans and has recently added other Spanish-speaking groups. (online by subscription, CD-ROM)

A Comprehensive Bibliography for the Study of American Minorities. 2 vols. 1976. Supplies annotated entries on resources about thirty-seven minority groups.

Ethnic News Watch. Indexes and supplies full articles from over eighty periodicals representing a wide range of ethnic viewpoints. (CD-ROM)

Guide to Research on North American Indians. 1983. Supplies annotated entries on articles, books, and government materials on a great variety of topics.

Hispanic American Periodicals Index (HAPI). 1970–. Indexes articles from about 250 periodicals treating Hispanic topics in Latin America and the United States. (online by subscription, CD-ROM)

Index to Black Periodicals. 1984–. Formerly *Index to Periodical Articles by and about Blacks,* 1971–83, and *Index to Periodical Articles by and about Negroes,* 1960–70. Indexes articles from periodicals.

Native Americans: An Annotated Bibliography. 1991. Lists articles and books, including those focused on a single tribe.

Women of Color in the United States: A Guide to the Literature. 1989. Supplies annotated entries on major resources.

WEB RESOURCES FOR ETHNIC STUDIES

Africa Web Links: An Annotated Resource List
<http://www.sas.upenn.edu/African_Studies/Home_Page/WWW_Links.html>
Supplies annotated links, multimedia archives, and other resources on African and black culture, arts, history, and issues.

The African-American Mosaic: A Library of Congress Resource Guide for the Study of Black History and Culture
<http://lcweb.loc.gov/exhibits/african/intro.html>
Samples information and images from the collections of the Library of Congress on colonization, abolition, migration, and the WPA.

Ancestors in the Americas
<http://www.cetel.org/>
Devoted to publishing and producing resources in the area of multiculturalism, with a special emphasis on Asian and Asian American concerns.

CLNet (Chicano-Latino Network)
<http://latino.sscnet.ucla.edu>
Includes links to Chicano and Latino research, curricula, regional information, data, and other information.

The International Institute
<http://www.umich.edu/~iinet/index.html>
Includes resources and links to other Web sites for many University of Michigan programs, such as African-American and African, Chinese, Japanese, Russian and Eastern European, and other international studies.

LANIC (Latin American Network Information Center)
<http://lanic.utexas.edu>
Provides access by country or topic to a great range of cultural, political, historical, economic, statistical, and other information for over twenty-five Latin American countries.

NativeWeb
 <http://www.nativeweb.org>
 Consolidates hundreds of links to resources, data, news, and information about events concerning native and indigenous peoples, organized by subject, country, and region.

The WWW Virtual Library: Asian Studies
 <http://coombs.anu.edu.au/wwwvl-AsianStudies.html>
 Contains a broad range of information and resources, including links to subject-oriented bibliographies on dozens of individual countries.

The WWW Virtual Library: Migration and Ethnic Relations
 <http://www.ercomer.org/wwwvl/>
 Provides an Interactive Information Board and links to research sites, academic institutions, publications, and other resources.

Geography

GENERAL REFERENCE SOURCES FOR GEOGRAPHY

Encyclopedia of Geographic Information Sources: U.S. Volume. 1987. Indexes sources by city, state, and area.

World Geographical Encyclopedia. 5 vols. 1995. Contains information on the environments, populations, economies, histories, and cultures of over 190 countries and a general study of geography and world statistics; arranged in volumes by continent and organized thematically within each volume.

INDEXES AND DATABASES FOR GEOGRAPHY

Geographical Abstracts: Physical Geography. 1989–. Formerly part of *Geological Abstracts: Paleontology & Stratigraphy.* Indexes and abstracts articles from over one thousand periodicals as well as books, papers, and reports on physical geography and cartography, including topics such as landforms, climatology, hydrology, and meteorology. (online by subscription as *GEOBASE*)

WEB RESOURCES FOR GEOGRAPHY

Colorado University: Resources for Geographers
<http://www.Colorado.edu/geography/virtdept/resources/contents.htm>
Provides resource lists, organized by topic; search engines; and links to journals, newsgroups, organizations, and other geography-related information.

Geographic Nameserver
<http://www.mit.edu:8001/geo>
Supplies information about places, primarily in the United States, including state, county, latitude, longitude, elevation, and population.

Manual of Federal Geographic Data Products: USGS Index
<http://www.fgdc.gov/FGDP/title.html>
Provides maps, photographs, and reports on topics such as mineral and energy resources, water and flood conditions, and earthquake information, plus links to resources from other federal agencies.

U.S. Gazetteer
<http://www.census.gov/cgi-bin/gazetteer>
Searches for locations in the United States, identifying them for viewing through the Tiger Map Server and for finding corresponding census data.

UT Austin Internet Resources for Geographers
<http://www.colorado.edu/geography/virtdept/resources/contents.htm>
Links to references, lists, journals, organizations, libraries, map collections, databases, and other resources in geography.

The WWW Virtual Library: Geography
<http://geography.pinetree.org>
Organizes linked resources, maps, databases of names, data, and other materials by subject, including countries and academic institutions.

Law and Criminal Justice

**GENERAL REFERENCE SOURCES FOR
LAW AND CRIMINAL JUSTICE**

Encyclopedia of Crime and Justice. 4 vols. 2002. Supplies articles, including reference lists, on major topics, including differing points of view.

Encyclopedia of the American Constitution. 4 vols. 2000. Contains long articles on laws, acts, decisions, notable figures, and historical periods, combining legal, historical, and political science viewpoints.

Encyclopedia of the American Judicial System: Studies of the Principal Institutions and Processes of Law. 3 vols. 1987. Supplies essays on legal history, processes, and issues.

Guide to American Law: Everyone's Legal Encyclopedia. 12 vols. 1985. Supplies definitions and extended articles on legal terms, topics, history, theory, and institutions, with an extensive appendix including sample forms, documents, and a time line.

The Oxford Companion to American Law. 2002. Contains 468 alphabetically arranged entries comprising biographies, concepts, current legal issues, definitions, descriptions of law enforcement agents and institutions, such as detectives and the FBI, and summaries of cases.

INDEXES AND DATABASES FOR LAW AND CRIMINAL JUSTICE

Current Law Index. 1980–. Indexes hundreds of law periodicals. (online by subscription, CD-ROM as *LegalTrac*)

Index to Legal Periodicals. 1908–. Indexes articles from over four hundred law periodicals. (online by subscription, CD-ROM)

WEB RESOURCES FOR LAW AND CRIMINAL JUSTICE

ABA Administrative Procedure Database
<http://www.law.fsu.edu/library/admin>
Contains links to state and federal Administrative Procedure Acts (APA), reform proposals, and other resources.

ASIL Guide to Electronic Resources for International Law
<http://www.asil.org/resource/Home.htm>
Sponsored by the American Society of International Law; provides advice on research and extensive links to all major areas of international law.

Internet Legal Resource Guide
<http://www.ilrg.com>
An extensive index, by category, of selected Web sites and files; designed for lay persons as well as legal scholars.

Justice Information Center: A Service of the National Criminal Justice Reference Service
<http://www.ncjrs.org>
Provides extensive information, statistics, and reports about criminal justice, crime prevention, courts, law enforcement, and related topics, with links to federal agencies, offices, and databases.

Law Library Research Exchange (LLRX)
<http://www.llrx.com/sources.html>
An award-winning search engine; provides up-to-date information and extensive links to a broad range of legal research and issues.

Legal Information Institute
<http://www.law.cornell.edu/>
A service of Cornell Law School: Access to recent and historic Supreme Court decisions and a hypertext version of all major federal laws. Good links to other central legal sites; allows searches.

U.S. Department of Justice
<http://www.usdoj.gov>
Supplies links to Department of Justice divisions, offices, and programs, as well as links to other federal and criminal justice sites.

The WWW Virtual Library: Law
<http://www.law.indiana.edu/v-lib>
Presents an extensive array of sites and resources, organized by legal specialty and topic, as well as by law school, legal firm, journal, government agency, and so on.

Political Science

GENERAL REFERENCE SOURCES FOR POLITICAL SCIENCE

Almanac of American Politics: The President, the Senators, the Representatives, the Governors: Their Records and Election Results, Their States and Districts. 1972–. Biennial. Analyzes state and national politics, including data and maps. (online by subscription)

Congressional Quarterly Almanac. 1945–. Analyzes national politics each year following the congressional session, including congressional legislation and voting records, presidential speeches, and Supreme Court decisions.

Political Handbook of the World. 1927–. Supplies current political information about individual countries and their connections through intergovernmental bodies.

State Legislative Sourcebook: A Resource Guide to Legislative Information in the 50 States. Annual. Lists publications and telephone numbers for state legislatures.

INDEXES AND DATABASES FOR POLITICAL SCIENCE

ABC Pol Sci: A Bibliography of Current Contents: Political Science and Government. 1969–. Supplies tables of contents from several hundred periodicals in political science, government, economics, law, and sociology. (CD-ROM)

Political Science: A Guide to Reference and Information Sources. 1990. Supplies annotated entries on political science sources, including databases, research collections, and organizations.

Population Index. 1935–. Supplies abstracts of periodical articles and other resources dealing with population theories, studies, research methods, statistics, and changes in patterns of birth, migration, and death.

United States Political Science Documents. 1975–. Indexes scholarly periodicals in political science. (online by subscription)

WEB RESOURCES FOR POLITICAL SCIENCE

Democratic Party Online
<http://www.democrats.org/>
The homepage of the Democratic National Committee, with useful links to party news, issues, and initiatives.

DTIC
<http://www.dtic.mil>
The Defense Technical Information Center is the U.S. military's own information service, with very detailed coverage of the Defense Technical Information Web and links to specific databases.

Fedworld
<http://www.fedworld.gov/>
Links to government services and databases. Good search facilities and explanations, with information on how to order materials.

The Gallup Organization
 <http://www.gallup.com/>
 Allows searches and includes up-to-date information and links to a variety of polling-related news items.

Political Resources on the Net
 <http://www.politicalresources.net>
 Contains political sites, organized by country, with links to parties, governments, organizations, and other political resources; allows searches.

Political Science Resources on the Web
 <http://www.lib.umich.edu/govdocs/polisci.html>
 Provides extensive annotated links and searches to many political sites and publications.

Political Science Virtual Library
 <http://lib.uconn.edu/PoliSci/polisci.htm>
 Links to departments, libraries, journals, government agencies, newsgroups and listservs, and related fields.

Republican Main Street
 <http://www.rnc.org/>
 The homepage of the Republican National Committee, with many useful links, not all to party issues.

Thomas: Legislative Information on the Internet
 <http://thomas.loc.gov/>
 The homepage of the U.S. Congress, with searches and links to current legislation, *Congressional Record* archives, historical documents, and other government resources.

United Nations
 <http://www.un.org/>
 A good general site, with links to many UN offices, policies, and activities. Also available in French and Spanish.

The White House
 <http://www.whitehouse.gov>
 The presidential site, with links to the president and vice president, commonly requested federal services, news, a virtual library, and other executive-branch links.

Psychology

GENERAL REFERENCE SOURCES FOR PSYCHOLOGY

The Corsini Encyclopedia of Psychology and Behavioral Science. 4 vols. 2002. Provides over 1,200 entries covering biographical information on important figures, the history of psychology, psychological theory, and concepts and techniques in areas such as applied, cognitive, educational, physiological, and social psychology.

Encyclopedia of Psychology. 8 vols. 2000. Supplies articles, along with reference lists, on many topics in psychology, including biographies of notable figures.

Oxford Companion to the Mind. 1987. Provides definitions and articles on topics and major figures in psychology, and includes other approaches to the mind as varied as the computer sciences, the fine arts, medicine, and traditional myths.

INDEXES AND DATABASES FOR PSYCHOLOGY

Bibliographic Guide to Psychology. 1974–. Comprehensively lists materials in all areas of psychology.

Mental Health Abstracts. 1969–. Formerly *NIMH Data Base.* Abstracts articles from over a thousand journals, as well as books and papers about mental health. (online by subscription)

Psychological Abstracts. 1927–. Indexes and abstracts articles from over fourteen hundred psychology periodicals, on many special topics such as developmental, educational, experimental, and social psychology. (online by subscription via *PsycINFO,* CD-ROM as *PsycLIT*)

WEB RESOURCES FOR PSYCHOLOGY

American Psychological Association
   <http://www.apa.org/>
   The APA homepage, with access to their online documents search tool, and information for students in psychology.

American Psychological Society
 <http://www.psychologicalscience.org>
 Links to journals, departments, Net resources and discussion groups, and research information.

Behavior Analysis Resources
 <http://typhoon.coedu.usf.edu/behavior/bares.htm>
 Links to resources in behavioral psychology.

Cognitive and Psychological Sciences on the Net
 <http://www-psych.stanford.edu/cogsci>
 Indexes resources on the Net that deal with research in cognition and psychology. Note that this site does not cover clinical psychology or mental health issues.

Freudnet: The Brill Library
 <http://plaza.interport.net/nypsan/>
 Includes psychoanalytic news, services, and links to electronic research.

Galaxy Psychology Page
 <http://galaxy.com/galaxy/Social-Sciences/Psychology.html>
 A large site divided into clinical, developmental, educational, experimental, and other lists. Also offers a search facility with links to academic organizations, collections, directories, and discussion groups.

Internet Mental Health
 <http://www.mentalhealth.com/main.html>
 Links to the most common mental disorders and medications, news, diagnosis, and help.

Neuropsychology Central
 <http://www.neuropsychology.com/index.html>
 Links to almost any aspect of neuropsychology.

PsychWeb
 <http://www.psywww.com>
 Contains helpful information and numerous links to psychology resources; geared to students and teachers.

Social Psychology Network
 <http://www.socialpsychology.org>
 The largest social-psychology database on the Internet; has search capability and links to more than 5,000 resources.

The Virtual Psychology Library
   <http://www-mugc.cc.monash.edu.au/psy/ol/psylinks.html>
   Good general links to major North American psychology sites.

Sociology and Social Work

GENERAL REFERENCE SOURCES FOR SOCIOLOGY AND SOCIAL WORK

Encyclopedia of Social Work. 3 vols. 1990. Supplies articles on social work, covering current issues such as adolescent behavior, divorce, homelessness, immigration, and welfare.

International Encyclopedia of Sociology. 2 vols. 1996. Contains 335 entries that illustrate the main topics and concerns in the field of sociology.

INDEXES AND DATABASES FOR SOCIOLOGY AND SOCIAL WORK

Social Work Research and Abstracts. 1977–. Indexes and abstracts resources related to social work. (online by subscription, CD-ROM)

Sociological Abstracts. 1952–. Indexes and abstracts articles, books, papers, and other resources on diverse topics, including the history, methods, and perspectives of the major fields in sociology. (online by subscription, CD-ROM as *SocioFile*)

WEB RESOURCES FOR SOCIOLOGY AND SOCIAL WORK

Annual Reviews of Sociology Online
   <http://www.annurev.org/>
   Allows searches of databases for downloadable abstracts.

Social Work and Social Services Web Sites
   <http://gwbweb.wustl.edu/websites.html>
   Provides information on abuse and violence, addiction, alternative medicine, emotional support, gender issues, and welfare.

Sociological Abstracts
<http://www.socabs.org/>
Provides links to other free sites in sociology.

A Sociological Tour through Cyberspace
<http://www.trinity.edu/~mkearl/index.html>
Provides links within sociology, including theory, data, methods, paper-writing guides, and inquiry help.

SocioSite
<http://www.pscw.uva.nl/sociosite>
A social science information system; allows searches and research in any sociological subject.

The Socioweb
<http://www.sonic.net/~markbl/socioweb/>
A general site of links and resources, including searches by topic.

Socioworld
<http://www.geocities.com/CollegePark/Library/8419/wbpthfnd.html>
Includes links to sociology journals, professional associations, listservs, and a sociology ring.

WWW Virtual Library—Sociology
<http://www.mcmaster.ca/socscidocs/w3virtsoclib/>
Links to sites covering research centers, discussion groups, e-journals, organizations, and university departments.

Women's Studies

GENERAL REFERENCE SOURCES FOR WOMEN'S STUDIES

Women's Studies Encyclopedia. 3 vols. 1999. Supplies articles on studies of women from the viewpoints of the natural sciences, the humanities, and the social sciences, including both historical background and recent research. (online by subscription)

INDEXES AND DATABASES FOR WOMEN'S STUDIES

Introduction to Library Research in Women's Studies. 1985. Supplies annotated source lists and guidance about research in this area.

Women's Studies Abstracts. 1972–. Indexes and abstracts articles from about three hundred periodicals, on topics such as education, employment, family, history, and sex roles. (online by subscription as part of *Women's Studies International*)

Women's Studies Index. 1989–. Indexes over one hundred periodicals in the field, including popular publications. (CD-ROM)

WEB RESOURCES FOR WOMEN'S STUDIES

The American Studies Web
<http://www.georgetown.edu/crossroads/asw>
Includes links to research sources for women's studies, among other topics in American studies.

International Gay and Lesbian Review
<http://www.usc.edu/archives/oneigla/onepress/index.html>
Provides abstracts and reviews of many books related to lesbian, gay, bisexual, and transgender studies.

Internet Gateway: Feminist Majority Foundation
<http://www.feminist.org/gateway/1_gatway.html>
Supplies links to selected Internet resources on women and women's issues.

Literary Resources—Feminism and Women's Literature
<http://newark.rutgers.edu/~jlynch/Lit/women.html>
Devoted entirely to women writers and feminist criticism.

The Women's Resource Project!
<http://www.ibiblio.org/chery6/women/wshome.html>
Provides links to academic programs in women's studies, other sites on a range of topics, and library resources.

Women's Studies Resources
<http://www.mith2.umd.edu/WomensStudies/>
Includes images, government documents, bibliographies, and other resources, as well as links to other sites and library collections.

APA Style

One of the most important documentation styles is that of the American Psychological Association (APA), which is widely used in psychology and other social sciences. For further reference on APA style, consult the following volume:

> American Psychological Association. *Publication Manual of the American Psychological Association.* 5th ed. Washington, D.C.: APA, 2001.

DIRECTORY TO APA STYLE

In-Text Citations

1. Author named in a signal phrase, *196*
2. Author named in a parenthetical reference, *197*
3. Two authors, *197*
4. Three to five authors, *198*
5. Six or more authors, *198*
6. Corporate or group author, *198*
7. Unknown author, *199*
8. Two or more authors with the same surname, *199*
9. Two or more sources within the same parenthetical reference, *199*
10. Specific parts of a source, *199*
11. Email, personal communication, *200*
12. World Wide Web document, *200*

Content Notes

List of References

INDENTATION STYLE

BOOKS

1. Book by one author, *203*
2. Book by two or more authors, *203*
3. Book by a corporate or group author, *203*
4. Book by an unknown author, *203*

(Continued)

BOOKS

5. Book prepared by an editor, *204*
6. Selection in a book with an editor, *204*
7. Translation, *204*
8. Edition other than the first, *204*
9. One volume of a multi-volume work, *204*
10. Article in a reference work, *204*
11. Republication, *205*
12. Government document, *205*
13. Two or more books by the same author(s), *205*

PERIODICALS

14. Article in a journal paginated by volume, *205*
15. Article in a journal paginated by issue, *206*
16. Article in a magazine, *206*
17. Article in a newspaper, *206*
18. Unsigned article, *206*
19. Editorial or letter to the editor, *206*
20. Review, *206*
21. Published interview, *207*
22. Two or more works by the same author in the same year, *207*

ELECTRONIC SOURCES

23. World Wide Web site, *208*
24. Article from an online periodical, *209*
25. Article or abstract from a database, *209*
26. Online government document, *210*
27. Posting to a discussion group, *211*
28. Email message or synchronous communication, *211*
29. FTP (file transfer protocol), telnet, or gopher site, *212*
30. Software or computer program, *212*

(Continued)

OTHER SOURCES

31. Technical or research reports and working papers, *212*
32. Paper presented at a meeting or symposium, unpublished, *213*
33. Unpublished dissertation, *213*
34. Poster session, *213*
35. Film, video, or DVD, *213*
36. Television program, single episode, *213*
37. Sound recording, *214*

A Student Research Essay, APA Style

APA Format for In-Text Citations

APA style requires parenthetical references in the text to document quotations, paraphrases, summaries, and other material from a source. These citations correspond to full bibliographic entries in a list of references at the end of the text.

1. AUTHOR NAMED IN A SIGNAL PHRASE

Generally, use the author's name in a signal phrase to introduce the cited material, and place the date, in parentheses, immediately after the author's name. For a quotation, the page number, preceded by *p.,* appears in parentheses after the quotation. For a long, set-off quotation, position the page reference in parentheses one space after the final punctuation.

```
Key (1983) has argued that the placement of women
in print advertisements is subliminally
important.
```

```
As Briggs (1970) observed, parents play an
important role in building children's self-esteem
because "children value themselves to the degree
that they have been valued" (p. 14).
```

For electronic texts or other works without page numbers, paragraph numbers may be used instead, preceded by the ¶ symbol or the abbreviation *para.*

```
Denes (1980, ¶ 1) claimed that psychotherapy
is an art that is "volatile, unpredictable,
standardless in its outcome, subjective in
its worth."
```

2. AUTHOR NAMED IN A PARENTHETICAL REFERENCE

When you do not name the author in your text, give the name and the date, separated by a comma, in parentheses at the end of the cited material.

```
One study has found that only 68% of letters
received by editors were actually published
(Renfro, 1979).
```

3. TWO AUTHORS

Use both names in all citations. Join the names with *and* in a signal phrase, but use an ampersand (&) instead in a parenthetical reference.

```
Murphy and Orkow (1985) reached somewhat
different conclusions by designing a study that
was less dependent on subjective judgment than
were previous studies.
```

```
A recent study that was less dependent on
subjective judgment resulted in conclusions
somewhat different from those of previous studies
(Murphy & Orkow, 1985).
```

4. THREE TO FIVE AUTHORS

List all the authors' names for the first reference.

```
Belenky, Clinchy, Goldberger, and Tarule (1986)
suggested that many women rely on observing and
listening to others as ways of learning about
themselves.
```

In any subsequent references, use just the first author's name plus *et al.* ("and others").

```
From this experience, observed Belenky et al.
(1986), women learn to listen to themselves
think, a step toward self-expression.
```

5. SIX OR MORE AUTHORS

Use only the first author's name and *et al.* ("and others") in every citation, including the first.

```
As Mueller et al. (1980) demonstrated, television
holds the potential for distorting and manipulating
consumers as free-willed decision makers.
```

6. CORPORATE OR GROUP AUTHOR

If the name of the organization or corporation is long, spell it out the first time you use it, followed by an abbreviation in brackets. In later references, use the abbreviation only.

First Citation

```
(Centers for Disease Control [CDC], 1990)
```

Later Citations

```
(CDC, 1990)
```

7. UNKNOWN AUTHOR

Use the title or its first few words in a signal phrase or in parentheses (in this example, a book's title is italicized).

```
The school profiles for the county substantiate
this trend (Guide to secondary schools, 2003).
```

8. TWO OR MORE AUTHORS WITH THE SAME SURNAME

If your list of references includes works by different authors with the same surname, include the authors' initials in each citation.

```
G. Jones (1994) conducted the groundbreaking
study of retroviruses.
```

9. TWO OR MORE SOURCES WITHIN THE SAME PARENTHETICAL REFERENCE

If you cite more than one source at once, list works in alphabetical order by author's surname, separated by semicolons; list works by the same author in chronological order, separated by commas.

```
(Chodorow, 2001; Gilligan, 2002)
(Gilligan, 1977, 2002)
```

10. SPECIFIC PARTS OF A SOURCE

Use abbreviations (*chap., p.,* and so on) in a parenthetical reference to name the part of a work you are citing.

```
Montgomery (1998, chap. 9) argued that his
research yielded the opposite results.
```

11. EMAIL AND OTHER PERSONAL COMMUNICATION

Cite any personal letters, email, electronic postings, telephone conversations, or interviews with the person's initial(s) and last name, with the identification *personal communication* and the date in a parenthetical reference. Note, however, that APA recommends not including personal communications in the reference list.

```
J. L. Morin (personal communication, October 14,
1999) supported the claims in her article with
new evidence.
```

12. WORLD WIDE WEB DOCUMENT

To cite a source found on the Web, use the author's name and date as you would for a print source, then indicate the chapter or figure name of the document, as appropriate. If the source's publication date is unknown, use *n.d.* (no date). To document a quotation, include paragraph numbers if page numbers are unavailable.

```
Shade argued the importance of "ensuring
equitable gender access to the Internet" (1993,
p. 6).
```

APA Format for Content Notes

APA style allows content notes for information you wish to include to expand or supplement your text. Indicate such notes in the text by superscript numerals. Type the notes themselves on a separate page after the last page of the text, under the heading "Footnotes," centered at the top of the page. Double-space all entries. Indent the first line of each note five to seven spaces, but begin subsequent lines at the left margin.

SUPERSCRIPT IN TEXT

```
The age of the children involved in the study was
an important factor in the selection of items for
the questionnaire.[1]
```

FOOTNOTE

```
    [1]Marjorie Youngston Forman and William Cole
of the Child Study Team provided great assistance
in identifying appropriate items.
```

APA Format for a List of References

The alphabetical list of the sources cited in your essay is called *References*. (If your instructor asks that you list everything you have read as background—not just the sources you cite—call the list *Bibliography*.) Here are some guidelines for preparing such a list:

- Start your list on a separate page after the text of your document but before any appendices or notes. Number each page, continuing the numbering of the text.
- Type the heading *References,* not underlined or italicized or in quotation marks, centered one inch from the top of the page.
- Double-space, and begin your first entry. Unless your instructor suggests otherwise, do not indent the first line of each entry, but indent subsequent lines one-half inch or five spaces. Double-space the entire list.
- List sources alphabetically by authors' (or editors') last names. If a source has no known author or editor, alphabetize it by the first major word of the title, disregarding *A, An,* or *The.* If the list includes two or more works by the same author, see the examples on pages 205 and 207.

For source materials from books and periodicals, APA style specifies the treatment and placement of four basic elements—author, publication date, title, and publication information. Each element is followed by a period.

- *Author.* List *all* authors last name first, and use only initials for first and middle names. Separate the names of multiple authors with commas, and use an ampersand before the last author's name.
- *Publication date.* Enclose the date in parentheses. Use only the year for books and journals; use the year, a comma, and the month or month and day for magazines. Do not abbreviate the month.
- *Title.* Italicize titles and subtitles of books and periodicals. Do not enclose titles of articles in quotation marks. For books and articles, capitalize only the first word of the title and subtitle and any proper nouns or proper adjectives. Capitalize all major words in a periodical title.
- *Publication information.* For a book, list the city of publication (and the country or postal abbreviation for the state if the city is unfamiliar), a colon, and the publisher's name, dropping any *Inc., Co.,* or *Publishers.* For a periodical, follow the periodical title with a comma, the volume number (italicized), the issue number (if appropriate) in parentheses and followed by a comma, and the inclusive page numbers of the article. For newspaper articles and for articles and chapters in books, include the abbreviations *p.* ("page") or *pp.* ("pages").

If you are using software (Microsoft Word, EndNote, Research Assistant) to record and create a list of references, double-check that all formatting is accurate.

Indentation Style

The following sample entries are in a hanging indent format, where the first line aligns on the left and the subsequent lines indent one-half inch or five spaces. This is the customary APA format for final copy, including student papers. Unless your instructor suggests otherwise, it is the format we recommend. Note, however, that for manuscripts being submitted to journals, APA requires the reverse

APA Format for a List of References 203

(first lines indented, subsequent lines aligned on the left), assuming that it will be converted by a typesetting system to a hanging indent.

Books

1. BOOK BY ONE AUTHOR

Lightman, A. P. (2002). *The diagnosis.* New York: Vintage Books.

2. BOOK BY TWO OR MORE AUTHORS

Newcombe, F., & Ratcliffe, G. (1978). *Defining females--The nature of women in society.* New York: Wiley.

3. BOOK BY A CORPORATE OR GROUP AUTHOR

Institute of Financial Education. (1983). *Income property lending.* Homewood, IL: Dow Jones-Irwin.

Use the word *Author* as the publisher when the organization is both the author and the publisher.

American Chemical Society. (1978). *Handbook for authors of papers in American Chemical Society publications.* Washington, DC: Author.

4. BOOK BY AN UNKNOWN AUTHOR

National Geographic atlas of the world. (1999). Washington, DC: National Geographic Society.

5. BOOK PREPARED BY AN EDITOR

Hardy, H. H. (Ed.). (1998). *The proper study of mankind.* New York: Farrar, Straus.

6. SELECTION IN A BOOK WITH AN EDITOR

West, C. (1992). The postmodern crisis of the black intellectuals. In L. Grossberg, C. Nelson, & P. Treichler (Eds.), *Cultural studies* (pp. 689-705). New York: Routledge.

7. TRANSLATION

Durkheim, E. (1957). *Suicide* (J. A. Spaulding & G. Simpson, Trans.). Glencoe, IL: Free Press of Glencoe.

8. EDITION OTHER THAN THE FIRST

Kohn, M. L. (1977). *Class and conformity: A study in values* (2nd ed.). Chicago: University of Chicago Press.

9. ONE VOLUME OF A MULTIVOLUME WORK

Baltes, P., & Brim, O. G. (Eds.). (1980). *Life-span development and behavior* (Vol. 3). New York: Basic Books.

10. ARTICLE IN A REFERENCE WORK

Ochs, E. (1989). Language acquisition. In *International encyclopedia of communications*

```
        (Vol. 2, pp. 390-393). New York: Oxford
        University Press.
```

If no author is listed, begin with the title.

11. REPUBLICATION

```
Piaget, J. (1952). The language and thought of
        the child. London: Routledge & Kegan Paul.
        (Original work published 1932)
```

12. GOVERNMENT DOCUMENT

```
U.S. Census Bureau. (1975). Historical statistics
        of the United States, colonial times to
        1970. Washington, DC: U.S. Government
        Printing Office.
```

13. TWO OR MORE BOOKS BY THE SAME AUTHOR(S)

List two or more books by the same author in chronological order. Repeat the author's name in each entry.

```
Goodall, J. (1991). Through a window. Boston:
        Houghton-Mifflin.
Goodall, J. (1999). Reason for hope: A spiritual
        journey. New York: Warner Books.
```

Periodicals

14. ARTICLE IN A JOURNAL PAGINATED BY VOLUME

```
Shuy, R. (1981). A holistic view of language.
        Research in the Teaching of English, 15,
        101-111.
```

15. ARTICLE IN A JOURNAL PAGINATED BY ISSUE

Maienza, J. G. (1986). The superintendency:
 Characteristics of access for men and women.
 Educational Administration Quarterly, 22(4),
 59-79.

16. ARTICLE IN A MAGAZINE

Quinn, J. B. (2002, September 16). Bonds for
 beginners. *Newsweek,* 45.

17. ARTICLE IN A NEWSPAPER

Browne, M. W. (1988, April 26). Lasers for the
 battlefield raise concern for eyesight. The
 New York Times, pp. C1, C8.

18. UNSIGNED ARTICLE

What sort of person reads *Creative Computing*?
 (1985, August). *Creative Computing, 8,* 10.

19. EDITORIAL OR LETTER TO THE EDITOR

Russell, J. S. (1994, March 27). The language
 instinct [Letter to the editor]. *The New
 York Times Book Review,* p. 27.

20. REVIEW

Larmore, C. E. (1989). [Review of the book
 Patterns of moral complexity]. *Ethics, 99,*
 423-426.

21. PUBLISHED INTERVIEW

McCarthy, E. (1968, December 24). [Interview with
 Boston Globe Washington staff]. *Boston
 Globe,* p. B27.

22. TWO OR MORE WORKS BY THE SAME AUTHOR IN THE SAME YEAR

List two or more works by the same author published in the same year alphabetically, and place lowercase letters (*a, b,* etc.) after the dates.

Murray, F. B. (1983a). Equilibration as cognitive
 conflict. *Developmental Review, 3,* 54-61.
Murray, F. B. (1983b). Learning and development
 through social interaction. In L. Liben
 (Ed.), *Piaget and the foundations of
 knowledge* (pp. 176-201). Hillsdale, NJ:
 Erlbaum.

Electronic Sources

The *Publication Manual of the American Psychological Association,* fifth edition, includes guidelines for citing various kinds of electronic resources, including Web sites; articles, reports, and abstracts; some types of online communications; and computer software. Updated guidelines are maintained at the APA's Web site, <www.apa.org>.

The basic entry for most sources you access via the Internet should include the following elements:

- *Author.* Give the author's name, if available.
- *Publication date.* Include the date of Internet publication or of the most recent update, if available. Use *n.d.* (no date) when the publication date is unavailable.

- *Title.* List the title of the document or subject line of the message, neither underlined nor in quotation marks.
- *Publication information.* For documents from reference databases or scholarly projects, give the city of the publisher or sponsoring organization, followed by the name. For articles from online journals or newspapers, follow the title with a comma, the volume number (italicized), the issue number (if appropriate) in parentheses and followed by a comma, and the inclusive page numbers of the article.
- *Retrieval information.* For most Internet sources, type the word *Retrieved* followed by the date of access, followed by a comma. End with the URL or other retrieval information and no period. For listserv or newsgroup messages and other online postings, type *Message posted to,* followed by the name of the list or group, and archive information if appropriate.

23. WORLD WIDE WEB SITE

To cite a whole site, give the address in a parenthetical reference. To cite a document from a Web site, include information as you would for a print document, followed by a note on its retrieval.

```
American Psychological Association. (2000).
    DotComSense: Commonsense ways to protect
    your privacy and assess online mental health
    information. Retrieved January 25, 2001,
    from http://helping.apa.org/dotcomsense/
Mullins, B. (1995). Introduction to Robert Hass.
    Readings in Contemporary Poetry at Dia
    Center for the Arts. Retrieved April 24,
    1997, from http://www.diacenter.org/prg/
    poetry/95_96/intrhass.html
```

If no author is identified, give the title of the document followed by the date (if available), publication information, and retrieval statement.

```
Media images can spur eating disorders in teens.
     (2000, February 16). InteliHealth. Retrieved
     June 29, 2001, from http://www.intelihealth
     .com/IH/ihtIH/WSIHW000/333/8014/269144.html
```

24. ARTICLE FROM AN ONLINE PERIODICAL

If the article also appears in a print journal, no retrieval statement is required; instead, include the label *[Electronic version]* after the article title. However, if the online article is a revision of the print document (if the format differs or page numbers are not indicated), include the date of access and URL.

```
Palmer, K. S. (2000, September 12). In academia,
     males under a microscope. Washington Post.
     Retrieved January 23, 2001, from
     http://www.washingtonpost.com
Steedman, M., & Jones, G. P. (2000). Information
     structure and the syntax-phonology interface
     [Electronic version]. Linguistic Inquiry,
     31, 649-689.
```

To cite an online article that did not appear in print, give the date of access and URL.

```
Taylor, J. (1998, June). Constructing the
     relational mind. Psyche, 4(10). Retrieved
     August 11, 2001, from http://psyche.cs
     .monash.edu.au/v4/psyche-4-10-taylor.html
```

25. ARTICLE OR ABSTRACT FROM A DATABASE

Give the information as you would for a print document. List the date you retrieved the article and only the name of the database; you do not need to specify whether you accessed the database through an online library or personal service, the Web, or a CD-ROM. If you are citing an abstract, end by typing *Abstract retrieved* and the date of access and name of the database. End with the document number in parentheses, if appropriate.

```
Hayhoe, G. (2001). The long and winding road:
     Technology's future. Technical
     Communication, 48(2), 133-145. Retrieved
     September 22, 2001, from ProQuest database.
McCall, R. B. (1998). Science and the press: Like
     oil and water? American Psychologist, 43(2),
     87-94. Abstract retrieved August 23, 2002,
     from PsycINFO database (1988-18263-001).
Pryor, T., & Wiederman, M. W. (1998). Personality
     features and expressed concerns of
     adolescents with eating disorders.
     Adolescence, 33, 291-301. Retrieved August
     26, 2002, from Electric Library database.
```

26. ONLINE GOVERNMENT DOCUMENT

Cite an online government document as you would a printed government work, adding the date of access, and the URL. If there is no date, use *n.d.*

```
Finn, J. D. (1998, April). Class size and
     students at risk: What is known? What is
     next? Retrieved September 5, 2002, from
     United States Department of Education Web
     site http://www.ed.gov/pubs/ClassSize/
     title.html
```

```
United States Department of Education. (n.d.).
    Progress of education in the United States
    of America: 1990 through 1994. Retrieved
    September 5, 2002, from http://www.ed.gov
    /pubs/Prog95/index.html
```

27. POSTING TO A DISCUSSION GROUP

List an online posting in the references list only if you are able to retrieve the message from a mailing list's archive. Provide the author's name; the date of posting, in parentheses; and the subject line from the posting. Include any information that further identifies the message in square brackets. For a listserv message, end with the retrieval statement, including the name of the list and the URL of the archived message.

```
Troike, R. C. (2001, June 21). Buttercups and
    primroses [Msg 8]. Message posted to the
    American Dialect Society's ADS-L electronic
    mailing list, archived at http://listserv
    .linguistlist.org/archives/ads-l.html
```

For a newsgroup posting, end with the name of the newsgroup. (If the author's real name is unavailable, include the screen name.)

```
Wittenberg, E. (2001, July 11). Gender and the
    Internet [Msg 4]. Message posted to
    news://comp.edu.composition
```

28. EMAIL MESSAGE OR SYNCHRONOUS COMMUNICATION

Because the APA stresses that any sources cited in your list of references be retrievable by your readers, you should not include entries for email messages or synchronous communications (MOOs, MUDs);

instead, cite these sources in your text as forms of *personal communication* (see page 200).

29. FTP (FILE TRANSFER PROTOCOL), TELNET, OR GOPHER SITE

After the retrieval statement, give the address (substituting *ftp, telnet,* or *gopher* for *http* at the beginning of the URL) or the path followed to access information, with slashes to indicate menu selections.

```
Korn, P. (1994, October). How much does breast
     cancer really cost? Self. Retrieved May 5,
     1997, from gopher://nysernet.org:70/00/
     BCIC/Sources/SELF/94/how-much
```

30. SOFTWARE OR COMPUTER PROGRAM

Begin with the author's name only when an author is listed as owner of the software.

```
McAfee Office 2000. Version 2.0 [Computer
     software]. (1999). Santa Clara, CA: Network
     Associates.
```

Other Sources

31. TECHNICAL OR RESEARCH REPORTS AND WORKING PAPERS

```
Wilson, K. S. (1986). Palenque: An interactive
     multimedia optical disc prototype for
     children (Working Paper No. 2). New York:
     Center for Children and Technology, Bank
     Street College of Education.
```

APA Format for a List of References 213

32. PAPER PRESENTED AT A MEETING OR SYMPOSIUM, UNPUBLISHED

Cite the month of the meeting, if it is available.

Engelbart, D. C. (1970, April). *Intellectual
    implications of multi-access computing.*
    Paper presented at the meeting of the
    Interdisciplinary Conference on Multi-Access
    Computer Networks, Washington, DC.

33. UNPUBLISHED DISSERTATION

Leverenz, C. A. (1994). *Collaboration and
    difference in the composition classroom.*
    Unpublished doctoral dissertation, Ohio
    State University, Columbus.

34. POSTER SESSION

Ulman, H. L., & Walborn, E. (1993, March).
    Hypertext in the composition classroom.
    Poster session presented at the Annual
    Conference on College Composition and
    Communication, San Diego, CA.

35. FILM, VIDEO, OR DVD

Hitchcock, A. (Producer & Director). (1954). *Rear
    window* [Film]. Los Angeles: MGM.

36. TELEVISION PROGRAM, SINGLE EPISODE

Imperioli, M. (Writer), & Buscemi, S. (Director).
    (2002, October 20). *Everybody hurts*

```
[Television series episode]. In D. Chase
    (Executive Producer), The Sopranos. New
    York: Home Box Office.
```

37. SOUND RECORDING

Begin with the writer's name, followed by the date of copyright. At the end of the entry, give the recording date if it is different from the copyright date. Use parentheses for this date but no period.

```
Colvin, S. (1991). I don't know why. [Recorded by
    A. Krauss and Union Station]. On Every time
    you say goodbye [Cassette]. Cambridge, MA:
    Rounder Records. (1992)
```

A Student Research Essay, APA Style

The following essay was written for a communications class in which the author and a group of her peers had completed a substantial collaborative project on parking problems on campus. In carrying out this project, the group designed and conducted a survey of students who used parking services and interviewed business owners in the surrounding area to find out how the lack of campus parking affected them. The group presented their research findings in class and then carried out one more assignment: to write individual reports, describing what they had learned about small-group dynamics as a result of their project. Although the following essay is not a formal social-science research report, it does conform to the APA style of documentation. For additional sample APA research essays, go to <http://www.bedfordstmartins.com/smhandbook> and click on Student Samples.

Leadership Roles in a Small-Group Project
Merlla McLaughlin
Professor Bushnell
Communications 102
February 22, 2003

Leadership Roles 2

Abstract

Using the interpersonal communications research of J. K. Brilhart and G. J. Galanes, and W. Wilmot and J. Hocker, along with T. Hartman's personality assessment, I observed and analyzed the leadership roles and group dynamics of my project collaborators in a communications course. Based on results of the Hartman personality assessment, I predicted that a single leader would emerge. However, complementary individual strengths and gender differences encouraged a distributed leadership style, in which the group experienced little confrontation and conflict. Conflict, because it was handled positively, was crucial to the group's progress.

Leadership Roles in a Small-Group Project

College lectures provide students with volumes of information. Many experiences, however, cannot be understood well solely by *learning about* them in a classroom. Instead, these experiences can only be understood by *living* them. So it is with the workings of a small, task-focused group. What observations would I make after working with a group of peers on a class project? And what have I learned personally as a result of my involvement with our collaborative project?

Leadership Expectations and Emergence

Our six group members were selected by the instructor; half were male and half were female. We had already performed the Hartman Personality Assessment (Hartman, 1998) in class, an assessment that can also be found online (Hayden). Hartman has associated key personality traits with the colors red, blue, white, and yellow (see Table 1).

The assessment identified most of us as "Blues," concerned with intimacy and caring. Because of the bold qualities associated with "Reds," I expected that Nate, our only "Red," might become our leader. (Kaari, the only

Table 1

Hartman's Key Personality Traits

Trait category	Color			
	Red	Blue	White	Yellow
Motive	Power	Intimacy	Peace	Fun
Strengths	Loyal to tasks	Loyal to people	Tolerant	Positive
Limitations	Arrogant	Self-righteous	Timid	Uncommitted

Note. Table is adapted from information found at *The Hartman Personality Profile*, by N. Hayden. Retrieved February 15, 2003, from http://students.cs.byu.edu/~nhayden/Code/index.php

"White," seemed poised to become the peacekeeper if need be.) However, after Nate missed the first two meetings, it seemed that Pat, who contributed often during our first three real meetings, might emerge as leader. Pat has strong communications skills, and he is a tall male (and thus a commanding presence). Pat is also sensitive to others. I was somewhat surprised, then, when our group developed a distributed style of leadership (Brilhart & Galanes, 1998). The longer we worked together, however, the more convinced I became that this approach to leadership was best for our group.

Leadership Roles 5

As Brilhart and Galanes have noted, "distributed leadership explicitly acknowledges that the leadership of a group is spread among members, with each member expected to perform the communication behaviors needed to move the group toward its goal" (p. 175). These researchers have divided positive communicative actions into two types: task functions that affect a group's productivity, and maintenance functions that influence the interactions of group members. Our group members enacted many task- and maintenance-focused communication roles. One of our most immediate task-function needs was decision-making, and as we made our first major decision--what topic to pursue--our group's distributed-leadership style began to emerge.

Decision-Making Methods

Our decision to do an investigative report on the parking services at Oregon State University (OSU) was not the result of a majority vote but was achieved instead through negotiated consensus. Nate was absent on the day we made our decision, but we felt that we needed to move from brainstorming--which we had already done--to action. Several of us argued that a presentation on parking services at OSU would interest most students, and after more discussion the others

Leadership Roles 6

agreed. At our next meeting, Nate seemed happy to go along with our collaborative decision.

Although we spent a good deal of time debating the topic for our project, once we decided on one, other decisions came naturally. At one point, for instance, we considered producing a videotape for part of our final presentation to the class. But after we discussed whether we had the resources and skills to shoot, edit, and produce a videotape, we quickly realized that it was not feasible. By using slides instead (which Pat and Nate prepared), we were still able to tie the whole presentation together through visual images.

Roles Played

Thanks in part to the distributed leadership that our group developed, the strengths of individual group members became increasingly apparent. While early in our project Pat had been the key initiator and Nate had acted largely as an information seeker, all group members eventually took on these task functions. We took turns serving as recorders, and we all gathered information and worked on our questionnaire. McKenzie, Kaari, Pat, and I all coordinated the group's work at some point. Kaari, Joe, and I

Leadership Roles 7

traded off as gatekeeper--the role of ensuring that everyone could speak and be heard. Joe was especially good at catching important details the rest of us were apt to miss. At one meeting, for instance, he pointed out that parking problems on campus could affect surrounding businesses and that interviewing business owners and employees could be informative. Joe, McKenzie, Kaari, and I frequently clarified or elaborated on information. Pat, Kaari, and Nate were particularly good at contributing ideas during brainstorming sessions. Nate, Joe, and McKenzie kept humor in the group by providing tension-relieving jokes and dramatic "what if" scenarios.

Just as each group member brought individual strengths to the group, gender differences also made us effective as a whole. For example, the women all seemed to take a holistic approach to the project--to look at the big picture--and to make intuitive leaps in ways that the men generally did not. The men preferred a more systematic process. Brilhart and Galanes have suggested that men working in groups dominated by women may display "subtle forms of resistance to a dominant presence of women" (p. 98). Although the men in our group did not attend all the meetings and the women did, I do not believe that the men's nonattendance implied male resistance any more than the women's attendance implied female dominance. Our differing qualities complemented each other and enabled us to work effectively as we conducted research, organized the information we gathered, and prepared for and gave a successful presentation.

Social Environment

As previously noted, our group primarily consisted of Blues, who value altruism, intimacy, appreciation, and having a moral conscience (Hayden, "Blues"). At least three of the four Blues had White as their secondary color; peace, kindness, independence, and sacrifice are important to Whites (Hayden, "Whites"). The presence of these traits may explain why our group had little confrontation and conflict. Nate, the Red, was most likely to speak bluntly, but everyone was careful to self-monitor during group interactions. The one time that Nate seemed put off, at the third meeting, it was not his words but his body language that expressed his discomfort. Nate sat at the far end of the group and leaned back in his chair with his arms crossed, his legs stretched out, and his ankles crossed. By contrast, everyone else in the group had scooted in close together. This was an awkward moment, but a rare one given our group's generally positive handling of conflict. Because obstacles were treated not as one person's problems but rather as a group problem, we approached difficulties from a united position instead of forming opposing camps among ourselves.

Conclusion

Perhaps my most important personal understanding as a result of this project has to do with conflict. I have always found conflict difficult and have believed, as Wilmot and Hocker (1998) have suggested, that most people think "harmony is normal and conflict is abnormal" (p. 9). Now I recognize that some kinds of conflict are essential for increasing understanding between group members and creating an effective collaborative product. It was essential, for instance, that our group explore different members' ideas about possible topics for our project, and this process inevitably required some conflict. The end result, however, was a positive one.

As Wilmot and Hocker have argued, conflict (in the sense of a discussion of multiple

Leadership Roles   10

possibilities) is essential to the full exploration of ideas. Good conflict, they say, requires an open and engaging attitude among group members and encourages personal growth. Good conflict ends when the issue at hand is resolved. And most important for our group, good conflict encourages cooperation (pp. 47-48). When group members handle conflict positively, they increase the group's cohesiveness. I think all the members of our group felt, for instance, that their ideas about possible topics were considered. Once we decided on a topic, everyone fully committed to it. Thus our group identity was enhanced by constructive conflict.

As a result of this project, I have a better sense of when conflict is--and isn't--productive. My group used conflict productively when we hashed out our ideas, and we avoided the kind of conflict that creates morale problems and wastes time. I realize that each group operates somewhat differently. But with the grounding this class has provided, I feel more prepared to understand and participate in future small-group projects.

References

Brilhart, J. K., & Galanes, G. J. (1998). *Effective group discussion* (9th ed.). Boston: McGraw-Hill.

Hartman, T. (1998). *The color code: A new way to see yourself, your relationships, and your life.* New York: Scribner.

Hayden, N. (n.d.). *The Hartman Personality Profile.* Retrieved February 15, 2003, from http://students.cs.byu.edu/~nhayden/Code/index.php

Wilmot, W., & Hocker, J. (1998). *Interpersonal conflict* (5th ed.). Boston: McGraw-Hill.

7

Research in the Natural and Physical Sciences and in Mathematics

Resources in the Natural and Physical Sciences and in Mathematics

GENERAL REFERENCE SOURCES FOR THE NATURAL AND PHYSICAL SCIENCES AND FOR MATHEMATICS

CRC Handbook of Chemistry and Physics. 1913–. Supplies frequently used formulas, constants, properties of elements and compounds, atomic weights, and numerous illustrative charts and tables for reference. (online by subscription)

Encyclopedia of Physical Sciences and Technology. 18 vols. 2001. Supplies extensive articles on topics in the physical sciences and technology, including bibliographies, glossaries, and illustrations.

McGraw-Hill Dictionary of Scientific and Technical Terms. 1989. Supplies pronunciations and definitions for thousands of terms used in the pure and applied sciences. (CD-ROM)

McGraw-Hill Encyclopedia of Science and Technology. 20 vols. 2002. Supplies articles with bibliographies and illustrations for extensive coverage of topics in all scientific fields, with updated coverage of the earth sciences, environmental studies, engineering, medicine, chemistry, and other rapidly developing fields; many smaller specialized McGraw-Hill scientific encyclopedias derive from this major work. (CD-ROM supplies a concise edition)

Van Nostrand's Scientific Encyclopedia. 2 vols. 1995. Supplies articles explaining and defining a wide variety of terms and topics in the sciences, medicine, and mathematics.

INDEXES AND DATABASES FOR THE NATURAL AND PHYSICAL SCIENCES AND FOR MATHEMATICS

Abstracts and Indexes in Science and Technology: A Descriptive Guide. 1985. Supplies detailed information on specialized abstracts and indexes available for the various scientific disciplines.

General Science Index. 1978–. Indexes and abstracts over one hundred periodicals covering the sciences, mathematics, medicine, environmental studies, and related topics. (online by subscription, CD-ROM)

Information Sources in Science and Technology. 1993. Annotated guide to general and specialized resources for seventeen scientific, medical, and technological disciplines.

Science and Technology Information Sourcebook. 1994. Annotated guide to resources for the major scientific fields.

Science Citation Index. 1955–. Indexes and abstracts (on CD-ROM) citations in articles from over three thousand scientific periodicals; entries allow tracing influence through the frequency of later citations by other researchers. (online by subscription as part of Web of Science)

WEB RESOURCES FOR THE NATURAL AND PHYSICAL SCIENCES AND FOR MATHEMATICS

EurekAlert! Your Global Gateway to Science, Medicine, and Technology News
<http://www.eurekalert.org>
Posts, under the sponsorship of the American Association for the Advancement of Science, news of scientific, medical, and technological research advances; also includes glossaries, dictionaries, and other reference materials for major scientific fields.

Infomine: Scholarly Internet Resource Collections
<http://infomine.ucr.edu>
Supplies indexed and annotated links to databases and other resources of academic interest in biology, medicine, mathematics, and the physical sciences.

New Scientist
<http://www.newscientist.com>
Supplies engaging annotated links to selected sites in many scientific fields, including specialized topics.

NIST (National Institute of Standards and Technology) Virtual Library
<http://nvl.nist.gov>
Includes extensive links to sites, databases, and journals in many fields, including biotechnology, chemistry, mathematics, computer science, engineering, and physics.

Science Online
<http://www.sciencemag.org>
Includes the online version of *Science,* published weekly by the American Association for the Advancement of Science, and free access to current news about scientific advances and career information.

The Webliography: Internet Subject Guides
<http://www.lib.lsu.edu/weblio.html>
Provides extensive annotated guides to Web resources in the sciences, including biology, chemistry, earth sciences, history of science, medicine, physics, and specialized fields.

(See also the resources listed for the applied sciences in Chapter 8.)

Astronomy

GENERAL REFERENCE SOURCES FOR ASTRONOMY

Encyclopedia of Astronomy and Astrophysics. 2001. Supplies extensive articles, including glossaries and bibliographies, on major topics in these fields. (online at <http://www.ency-astro.com/>)

INDEXES AND DATABASES FOR ASTRONOMY

Astronomy and Astrophysics Abstracts. 1969–. Formerly *Astronomisches Jahresbericht,* 1900–68. Indexes and abstracts articles from periodicals, books, papers, and other materials, extensively covering astronomy, space research, astrophysics, planets, stars, and related topics.

WEB RESOURCES FOR ASTRONOMY

The Astronomy Cafe: The Web Site for the Astronomically Disadvantaged
<http://itss.raytheon.com/cafe/cafe.html>
Provides varied resources about astronomy, including questions and answers for astronomers and space scientists, career information, and an extensive list of links to related sites.

The Astronomy Net
<http://www.astronomy.net>
Includes links to recent news stories and articles, as well as discussion groups and clubs.

AstroWeb: Astronomy/Astrophysics on the Internet
<http://www.cv.nrao.edu/fit/www/astronomy.html>
Provides one version of the AstroWeb, a collaborative database of over two thousand items available at several sites, here sorted by category including images, observations, data, publications, organizations, people, research specialties, and other resources.

NASA Web
<http://www.nasa.gov>
Covers the aerospace program, space and earth sciences, technology applications, and topics such as shuttles and space stations; also provides links to other NASA resources and images.

The*Star's Family of Astronomy and Related Resources—The Star Pages
<http://vizier.u-strasbg.fr/starsfamily.html>
Includes thousands of entries, including abbreviations, symbols, and personal Web pages, as well as links to many organizations and resources.

WebStars: Astrophysics in Cyberspace
<http://heasarc.gsfc.nasa.gov/docs/www_info/webstars.html>
Supplies engaging annotations and images for links to astronomy, the solar system, and space exploration.

The WWW Virtual Library: Astronomy and Astrophysics & AstroWeb
<http://webhead.com/wwwvl/astronomy>
Supplies an impressive range of links to resources, observatories, organizations, publications, data, and images in astronomy and related fields.

Chemistry

GENERAL REFERENCE SOURCES FOR CHEMISTRY

Kirk-Othmer Encyclopedia of Chemical Technology. 27 vols. 1991–. Supplies hundreds of articles on the properties and uses of chemical substances as well as on other topics related to chemical processes, methods, and technology. (online by subscription)

Van Nostrand Encyclopedia of Chemistry. 1984. Supplies articles on chemistry-related topics as diverse as food chemistry, plant chemistry, pollution, and energy sources.

INDEXES AND DATABASES FOR CHEMISTRY

Chemical Abstracts. 1907–. Indexes and abstracts articles from over fourteen thousand periodicals, as well as books, reports, and other materials covering all major chemical fields. (online by subscription)

Chemical Reviews. 1924–. 8/yr. Covers all areas of chemistry; includes comprehensive bibliographies. (online by subscription)

How to Find Chemical Information: A Guide for Practicing Chemists, Educators, and Students. 1998. Explains the contents of and ways to use major print and electronic resources in chemistry.

WEB RESOURCES FOR CHEMISTRY

ACSWEB
<http://www.acs.org/>
Provides searches of American Chemical Society resources as well as information on news, events, and publications.

Beginner's Guide to Chemical Abstracts
<http://library.uwaterloo.ca/howto/howto12.html>
Introduces users to the standard guide to chemical literature and shows how to do simple searches. A commercial site.

ChemCenter
<http://www.chemistry.org/>
From the American Chemical Society; includes links to education, industry, publications, and searchable databases.

CHEMINFO
 <http://www.indiana.edu/~cheminfo/cisindex.html>
 Chemical Information Sources from Indiana University is a guide to Internet and Web resources in chemistry; offers both alphabetical and keyword searches in a useful format.

Manual and Computer-Aided Literature Searching
 <http://www.brunel.ac.uk:8080/depts/chem/ch361a/lect.htm>
 A long, detailed explanation of how to use the standard sources in chemical literature, by Dr. J. J. Gosper. Includes a section on Beilstein and full explication of CA and BIDS. Worth downloading.

Molecular Visualization Tools and Sites
 <http://www.indiana.edu/~cheminfo/mvts.html>
 Links to all the major Chime and RasMol sites as well as to various other free and commercial visualization sites.

The WWW Virtual Library—Chemistry
 <http://www.liv.ac.uk/Chemistry/Links/links.html>
 Links to universities and organizations as well as to chemistry resources and other virtual libraries.

Earth Sciences

GENERAL REFERENCE SOURCES FOR EARTH SCIENCES

A Dictionary of Earth Sciences. 1999. Includes over 6,000 entries covering fields such as climatology, exonomic geology, geochemistry, oceanography, petrology, and volanology.

Encyclopedia of Earth Sciences. c. 24 vols. 1966–. Supplies articles in volumes focused on specific topics, including oceanography, mineralogy, paleontology, geology, climatology, and other specialized areas.

Encyclopedia of Earth System Science. 4 vols. 1992. Provides thorough coverage of topics in this specialized field.

Encyclopedia of Minerals. 1974–. Supplies descriptions and some color photographs of more than 2,500 minerals.

The Facts on File Dictionary of Earth Science. 2000. Lists general definitions of over 3,700 terms; includes cross-references.

Illustrated Dictionary of Earth Science. 2002. A CD-ROM containing over 8,700 definitions encompassing topics such as environmental science, physics, mining, and engineering, more than 2,000 of which are illustrated; all definitions and illustrations are printable.

McGraw-Hill Dictionary of Earth Sciences. 1997. Defines thousands of terms used in the various engineering fields, geology, mineralogy, crystallography, and paleontology.

McGraw-Hill Dictionary of Geology and Mineralogy. 1997. Contains over 7,000 terms and expressions, each arranged under the field of geology and mineralogy in which it is used, including physical and historical geology, plate tectonics, and petrology.

INDEXES AND DATABASES FOR EARTH SCIENCES

Bibliography and Index of Geology. 1969–. Formerly *Bibliography of North American Geology*, 1931–72, and *Bibliography and Index of Geology Exclusive of North America*, 1933–68. Indexes articles on many geological topics, supplying extensive coverage of the field. (online by subscription as GEO Ref, CD-ROM)

WEB RESOURCES FOR EARTH SCIENCES

CIESIN: Information for a Changing World
<http://www.ciesin.org>
Consolidates scientific data, interactive services, and access to resources on the global environment, under the auspices of the Consortium for International Earth Science Information Network.

Geologylink
<http://www.geologylink.com>
Provides, under the sponsorship of the publisher Houghton Mifflin, news, current events, visits to geologic sites, a forum on geology, and links to course materials, references, glossaries, and other Web sites.

Hawaii Center for Volcanology
<http://www.soest.hawaii.edu/GG/hcv.html>
Provides links to numerous volcano sites, including the Hawaiian Volcano Observatory, NASA's Virtually Hawaii project, and a virtual voyage to Puna Ridge, a volcanic ridge three miles under the sea.

Resources in the Natural and Physical Sciences and in Mathematics

Internet Resources in the Earth Sciences
<http://www.lib.berkeley.edu/EART/EarthLinks.html>
An annotated list of sites in the earth sciences and more specialized fields such as seismology, weather, and oceanography.

Journals of Earth Sciences
<http://pinti.geol.upsud.fr/Homepage/Journal.htm>
Not a journal but rather a list of more than 700 journals worldwide.

NASA's Global Change Master Directory (GCMD)
<http://gcmd.gsfc.nasa.gov>
Allows keyword searches and includes many links to other earth science sources.

National Geophysical Data Center
<http://www.ngdc.noaa.gov>
Supplies information—including satellite data—for environmental studies and specialized fields such as marine geology, glaciology, and paleoclimatology.

USGS (United States Geological Survey): Science for a Changing World
<http://www.usgs.gov>
Provides highlights, fact sheets, information on federal programs and initiatives, and access to extensive resources and databases on geology, biology, water resources, mapping, and related topics.

The WWW Virtual Library: Earth Sciences
<http://www.vlib.org/EarthScience.html>
Categorizes its numerous links by subject; includes many subdisciplines such as oceanography and meteorology.

Life Sciences

GENERAL REFERENCE SOURCES FOR LIFE SCIENCES

Encyclopedia of Bioethics. 2 vols. 1982. Includes articles on life science ethics, policies, legal issues, religious perspectives, and related issues.

Encyclopedia of Human Biology. 8 vols. 1997. Provides hundreds of extensive articles on biological topics as diverse as anthropology, biochemistry, ecology, genetics, and physiology.

The Encyclopedia of Mammals. 2001. Entries cover every living species of mammal; emphasize animal behavior, conservation, and ecology; and are accompanied by over 800 full-color illustrations.

Encyclopedia of Microbiology. 4 vols. 1992. Supplies thorough coverage of topics in this specialized field.

Grzimek's Animal Life Encyclopedia. 13 vols. 1972–74. Provides articles and illustrations on the various kinds of animal life.

Grzimek's Encyclopedia of Mammals. 5 vols. 1989. Supplies photographs and articles with bibliographies on mammal groups, including detailed coverage of many species.

Mammals: A Multimedia Encyclopedia. Supplies National Geographic illustrations and information about hundreds of mammals. (CD-ROM)

Oxford Dictionary of Natural History. 1985. Provides thousands of definitions and explanations about the various types of plants and animals, plus genetics, biochemistry, and earth sciences.

Walker's Mammals of the World. 2 vols. 1991. Supplies entries, many illustrated, on mammal types, and includes a bibliography of sources cited.

INDEXES AND DATABASES FOR LIFE SCIENCES

Biological Abstracts. 1926–. Indexes and abstracts articles from roughly 9,500 periodicals, comprehensively covering biology and biomedicine. (online by subscription as BIOSIS Previews, CD-ROM)

Biological and Agricultural Index. 1964–. Formerly *Agricultural Index*, 1916–64. Indexes over 250 periodicals covering a wide range of agricultural and biological topics such as animal husbandry, zoology, genetics, botany, food production, and environmental studies. (online by subscription, CD-ROM)

Cumulative Index to Nursing and Allied Health Literature. 1961–. Indexes and abstracts hundreds of periodicals on nursing and related health areas. (online by subscription, CD-ROM)

Index Medicus. 1899–1926; 1960–. Formerly *Quarterly Cumulative Index Medicus*, 1927–59. Indexes thousands of major medical and health care periodicals, excluding popular magazines. (online as *PubMed* at <http://www.ncbi.nlm.nih.gov/entrez/query.fcgi?db=PubMed>, CD-ROM in *MEDLINE*)

WEB RESOURCES FOR LIFE SCIENCES

Biosciences Index
   <http://mcb.harvard.edu/BioLinks.html>
   Allows searching by keyword and provides an alphabetical list of links for specialties within the biosciences.

Biosciences Web Resources
   <http://www.herts.ac.uk/lis/subjects/natsci/bio/bioweb>
   Includes links to sites in the biosciences, from biochemistry to physiology, as well as links to reference works, journals, magazines, and newsletters in the field.

Centers for Disease Control
   <http://ftp.cdc.gov/>
   The homepage of the famous virus hunters, with links to what they do, search facilities, other sites, and a wide range of useful government data.

Human Genome Project
   <http://www.nhgri.nih.gov/index.html>
   The homepage for this important research project; situated at the National Institutes of Health.

Links to the Genetic World
   <http://www.ornl.gov/hgmis/links.html>
   Provides basic and specialized information on genetics and the Human Genome Project, as well as keyword searches and links to numerous genetics-related sites.

National Institutes of Health
   <http://www.nih.gov/>
   The central government organization dealing with health issues; site includes news, health information, grant descriptions, and links to scientific resources and to NIH suborganizations.

National Science Foundation: Biology
   <http://www.nsf.gov/home/bio/>
   The site of the primary government agency funding scientific research. Allows a search of its Biology Directorate's sources and includes links to online documents, grants, and specific fields within biology.

NetVet
> <http://netvet.wustl.edu/vet/htm>
> From the Washington University Division of Comparative Medicine, includes links to special fields in veterinary medicine, numerous sites for particular animals, and an electronic zoo.

Nursing
> <http://www.atnursing.com>
> Allows keyword searches and includes annotated sites for nursing and other medical-related fields.

Pasteur Institute
> <http://web.pasteur.fr/search/>
> Allows keyword searches of the Pasteur Institute's server and many other English-language-based bioscience servers.

Scott's Botanical Links
> <http://www.ou.edu/cas/botany-micro/bot-linx>
> Includes annotated lists of databases and detailed descriptions of links to other botanical sites.

The WWW Virtual Library—Biosciences
> <http://vlib.org/Biosciences.html>
> Categorizes information by provider and subject. A good place to begin research, this site includes many links to journals, subdisciplines, and related sites.

(See also the resources listed for agriculture in Chapter 8 on the applied sciences.)

Mathematics

GENERAL REFERENCE SOURCES FOR MATHEMATICS

CRC Handbook of Mathematical Sciences. 1987. Supplies frequently used mathematical functions, equations, factors, formulas, measurements, statistics, and abbreviations.

Encyclopedic Dictionary of Mathematics. 4 vols. 1987. Includes articles defining many mathematical terms and topics.

Resources in the Natural and Physical Sciences and in Mathematics 237

INDEXES AND DATABASES FOR MATHEMATICS

Mathematical Reviews. 1940–. Indexes and abstracts extensive resources in all areas of mathematics, including theory, history, probability, games, circuits, and related topics. (online by subscription as *Math on the Web*, CD-ROM as *MathSciDisc*)

WEB RESOURCES FOR MATHEMATICS

American Mathematical Society, Mathematics on the Web
<http://www.ams.org/mathweb/>
Offers literature guides and links both on- and offline, references, topical guides, and links to individuals.

Eric's Treasure Trove of Mathematics
<http://mathworld.wolfram.com>
An alphabetical search list of important terms and concepts.

Materials Organized by Mathematical Topics
<http://www.ams.org/mathweb/mi-mathbytopic.html>
Links to specific issues in current mathematical work.

Math Archives Bibliographies
<http://archives.math.utk.edu/cgi-bin/bibliography.html>
Lists bibliographies and subject links; supplements the Math Archives homepage.

Math Archives Undergrads' Page
<http://archives.math.utk.edu/undergraduates.html>
Devoted to math issues of special interest to undergraduates. Includes societies, projects, research, competitions, and career issues.

Math Forum Internet Mathematics Library
<http://mathforum.org/library>
Provides extensive links to all areas of mathematics, including math education from elementary through college levels.

MathSearch
<http://www.maths.usyd.edu.au:8000/MathSearch.html>
Searches over ninety thousand documents on English-language math and statistics servers, keying by phrase.

The Most Common Errors in Undergraduate Mathematics
   <http://math.vanderbilt.edu/~schectex/commerrs/>
   From Eric Schecter at Vanderbilt University.

(See also the resources listed for engineering in Chapter 8 on the applied sciences.)

Physics

GENERAL REFERENCE SOURCES FOR PHYSICS

American Institute of Physics Handbook. 1972. Supplies formulas and other reference materials, specifically selected for the physicist.

Encyclopedia of Physics. 1991. Includes extensive articles written for a general audience on major topics in the field.

Handbook of Physics. 2002. Contains fundamental concepts, formulas, rules, theorems, and tables of standard values and material properties; topics discussed include classical mathematics, elementary particles, electric circuits, and error analysis.

McGraw-Hill Dictionary of Physics. 1997. Defines thousands of key terms from eighteen areas of physics and other closely connected fields.

INDEXES AND DATABASES FOR PHYSICS

Information Sources in Physics. 1985. Supplies entries on print and electronic resources in physics.

Physics Abstracts. 1898–. Indexes and abstracts periodicals and other resources in major areas of physics and in related scientific fields. (online by subscription, CD-ROM)

WEB RESOURCES FOR PHYSICS

AIP Physics Information
   <http://www.aip.org/>
   Links to societies, publications, career services, and databases from the American Institute of Physics.

American Physical Society
    <http://www.aps.org/>
    Allows quick access to professional activities and databases.

Contemporary Physics Education Project
    <http://www.cpepweb.org>
    Provides links to several interactive explanations of fields in physics, and lists of other sites.

HEPIC Global Search
    <http://www.hep.net/search/global.html>
    Covers all the major electronic databases in physics, using a keyword search.

The NASA Homepage
    <http://www.nasa.gov>
    Contains useful links to current NASA projects.

The Net Advance of Physics
    <http://www.mit.edu/afs/athena.mit.edu/user/r/e/redingtn/www/netadv/welcome.html>
    Includes the *Physicist's Encyclopedia*, a collection of review articles in physics arranged by subject.

Physics News
    <http://www.het.brown.edu/news/index.html>
    Lists the latest work being done in physics, including NASA's *Hot Topics* and the newsletter *The Scientist*, science news from wire services, and links to other journals and magazines.

Physicsweb
    <http://physicsweb.org/>
    Allows access to physics societies, databases, projects, news, and events.

PhysLink.com
    <http://www.physlink.com>
    Contains articles on current news items, links to journals and physics departments, and a question-and-answer feature.

U.S. Department of Energy
    <http://www.energy.gov/>
    Contains data on current research and developments in physics; subsidized by the Department of Energy.

The WWW Virtual Library—Physics
   <http://www.vlib.org/Physics.html>
   Categorizes its links by subject.

CBE Style

Many writers in the natural and physical sciences use the documentation style recommended by the Council of Science Editors (formerly the Council of Biology Editors, or CBE). For further reference on CBE style, consult the following volume:

   Council of Biology Editors. *Scientific Style and Format: The CBE Manual for Authors, Editors, and Publishers.* 6th ed. New York: Cambridge UP, 1994.

CBE Formats for In-Text Citations

In CBE style, citations within an essay follow one of two formats.

- The citation-sequence format calls for a superscript number ([1]) or a number in parentheses after any mention of a source.
- The name-year format calls for the last name of the author and the year of publication in parentheses after any mention of a source. If the last name appears in a signal phrase, the name-year format allows for giving only the year of publication in parentheses.

Dr. Edward Huth, chairperson of the Council of Science Editors' Style Manual Committee, recommends either the name-year or the superscript (citation-sequence format) system rather than the number-in-parentheses system—and suggests that student writers check a current journal in the field or ask an instructor about the preferred style in a particular course or discipline.

1. IN-TEXT CITATION USING CITATION-SEQUENCE SUPERSCRIPT FORMAT

```
In his lengthy text, Gilman[1] provides the most
complete discussion of this phenomenon.
```

For the citation-sequence format, you would also use a superscript ([1]) for each subsequent citation of this work by Gilman.

2. IN-TEXT CITATION USING NAME-YEAR FORMAT

```
In his lengthy text, Gilman provides the most
complete discussion of this phenomenon (1994).

Maxwell's two earlier studies of juvenile obesity
(1988, 1991) examined only children with
diabetes.

The classic examples of such investigations
(Morrow 1968; Bridger and others 1971; Franklin
and Wayson 1972) still shape the assumptions of
current studies.
```

CBE Formats for a List of References

The citations in the text of an essay correspond to items on a list called References. If you use the citation-sequence superscript format, number and list the references in the sequence in which the references are *first* cited in the text. If you use the name-year format, list the references, unnumbered, in alphabetical order.

In the following examples, you will see that the citation-sequence format calls for listing the date after the publisher's name in references for books and after the periodical name in references for articles.

The name-year format calls for listing the date immediately after the author's name in any kind of reference. Notice also the absence of a comma after the author's last name, the absence of a period after an initial, and the absence of underlining or italics in titles of books or journals.

If you are using software (Microsoft Word, EndNote, Research Assistant) to record and create a list of references, double-check that all formatting is accurate.

DIRECTORY TO CBE STYLE FOR A LIST OF REFERENCES

BOOKS

1. One author, *243*
2. Two or more authors, *243*
3. Organization as author, *243*
4. Book prepared by editor(s), *244*
5. Section of a book with an editor, *244*
6. Chapter of a book, *244*
7. Published proceedings of a conference, *245*

PERIODICALS

8. Article in a journal paginated by volume, *246*
9. Article in a journal paginated by issue, *246*
10. Article in a weekly journal, *246*
11. Article in a magazine, *246*
12. Article in a newspaper, *247*

ELECTRONIC SOURCES

13. Electronic books (monographs), *248*
14. Electronic journal articles, *249*
15. World Wide Web site, *249*
16. Material from an online database, *250*
17. Email, *250*
18. Posting to a discussion group, *250*

Books

For a book, the basic entry includes the following items: the author, with the last name first, no comma, and initials without periods for the first and middle names; the title, with only the first word and proper nouns and adjectives capitalized and without underlining, italics, or quotation marks; the place and year of publication; the publisher; and the number of pages in the book. Note the period at the end of each part of the entry.

1. ONE AUTHOR

[1]Freidson E. Profession of medicine. New York: Dodd-Mead; 1972. 802 p.

Freidson E. 1972. Profession of medicine. New York: Dodd-Mead. 802 p.

2. TWO OR MORE AUTHORS

[2]Stalberg E, Trontelj JV. Single fiber electromyography: studies in healthy and diseased muscle. New York: Raven; 1994. 291 p.

Stalberg E, Trontelj JV. 1994. Single fiber electromyography: studies in healthy and diseased muscle. New York: Raven. 291 p.

3. ORGANIZATION AS AUTHOR

Any organization abbreviation is placed at the beginning of the name-year entry and is used in the corresponding in-text citation.

³World Health Organization. World health
    statistics annual: 1993. Geneva: World
    Health Organization; 1994. 824 p.
[WHO] World Health Organization. 1994. World
    health statistics annual: 1993. Geneva: WHO.
    824 p.

4. BOOK PREPARED BY EDITOR(S)

⁴Berge ZL, Collins MP, editors. Computer mediated
    communication and the online classroom.
    Cresskill, NJ: Hampton Pr; 1995. 230 p.
Berge ZL, Collins MP, editors. 1995. Computer
    mediated communication and the online
    classroom. Cresskill, NJ: Hampton Pr. 230 p.

5. SECTION OF A BOOK WITH AN EDITOR

⁵Adler M. Stroke. In: Dulbecco R, editor.
    Encyclopedia of human biology. San Diego:
    Academic; 1991. p 299-308.
Adler M. 1991. Stroke. In: Dulbecco R, editor.
    Encyclopedia of human biology. San Diego:
    Academic. p 299-308.

6. CHAPTER OF A BOOK

⁶Castro J. The American way of health: how
    medicine is changing and what it means to
    you. Boston: Little, Brown; 1994. Chapter 9,

```
          Why doctors, hospitals, and drugs cost so
          much; p 131-53.
Castro J. 1994. The American way of health: how
          medicine is changing and what it means to
          you. Boston: Little, Brown. Chapter 9, Why
          doctors, hospitals, and drugs cost so much;
          p 131-53.
```

7. PUBLISHED PROCEEDINGS OF A CONFERENCE

```
[7][Anonymous]. International Conference on the Bus
          '86; 1986 Sep 9-10; London. [London]:
          Institution of Mechanical Engineers; 1986.
          115 p.
```

The place of publication was not stated but inferred and placed in brackets.

```
[Anonymous]. 1986. International Conference on
          the Bus '86; 1986 Sep 9-10; London.
          [London]: Institution of Mechanical
          Engineers. 115 p.
```

Periodicals

For a journal article, the basic entry includes the author, with the last name first, no comma, and initials without periods for the first and middle names; the article title, with only the first word and proper nouns and adjectives capitalized; the journal title, abbreviated; the date of the issue; the volume number; the issue number, if any; and the inclusive page numbers. For newspaper and magazine articles, the entry includes the section designation and column number, if any.

For rules on abbreviating journal titles, consult *The CBE Manual,* or ask an instructor or librarian to refer you to other examples. Following are examples using both superscript and name-year systems:

8. ARTICLE IN A JOURNAL PAGINATED BY VOLUME

[8]Finkel MJ. Drugs of limited commercial value. New Engl J Med 1980;302:643-4.

Finkel MJ. 1980. Drugs of limited commercial value. New Engl J Med 302:643-4.

9. ARTICLE IN A JOURNAL PAGINATED BY ISSUE

[9]Fagan R. Characteristics of college student volunteering. J Vol Admin 1992;11(1):5-18.

Fagan R. 1992. Characteristics of college student volunteering. J Vol Admin 11(1):5-18.

10. ARTICLE IN A WEEKLY JOURNAL

[10]Kerr RA. How many more after Northridge? Science 1994 Jan 28;263(5146):460-1.

Kerr RA. 1994 Jan 28. How many more after Northridge? Science 263(5146):460-1.

11. ARTICLE IN A MAGAZINE

[11]Jackson R. Arachnomania. Natural History 1995 Mar:28-31.

Jackson R. 1995 Mar. Arachnomania. Natural History:28-31.

12. ARTICLE IN A NEWSPAPER

[12]Christopher T. Grafting: playing Dr.
    Frankenstein in the garden. New York Times
    1995 Feb 19;Sect Y:21(col 1).

Christopher T. 1995 Feb 19. Grafting: playing Dr.
    Frankenstein in the garden. New York
    Times;Sect Y:21(col 1).

Electronic Sources

Although the 1994 edition of *The CBE Manual* includes a few examples for citing electronic sources, the Council of Science Editors now recommends the guidelines provided at its Web site, <www.councilscienceeditors.org/pubs_citing_internet.shtml>. The following formats are adapted from the advice on this site. The examples shown follow the citation-sequence format, but you can easily adapt them to the name-year format.

The basic entry for most sources you access through the Internet should include the following elements:

- *Author.* Give the author's name, if available, last name first, followed by the initial(s) and a period.
- *Title.* For book, journal, and article titles, follow the style for print materials. For all other types of electronic material, reproduce the title as closely as possible to the wording that appears on the screen.
- *Medium.* Indicate, in brackets, that the source is not in print format by using designations such as *[Internet]* or *[database on the Internet]*.
- *Place of publication.* The city usually should be followed by the two-letter abbreviation for state. If the city is inferred, put the city and state in brackets, followed by a colon. If the city cannot be inferred, use the words *place unknown* in brackets, followed by a colon. Note that very well-known cities, such as New York or Chicago, may be listed without a state designation.

- *Publisher.* Include the individual or organization that produces or sponsors the work or site. It is sometimes helpful to include a designation for country, in parentheses, after the publisher's name. If no publisher can be determined, use the words *publisher unknown* in brackets.
- *Dates.* Cite three important dates if possible: the date the publication was placed on the Internet or was copyrighted; the latest date of any update or revision; and the date the publication was accessed by you. Dates should be expressed in the format "year month day," and the date of copyright should be preceded by a *c* as in *c2000*. (Because several dates are preferred in citations from electronic sources, the following examples group all dates together after the publisher's name. Since this style is different from what is done with most print materials, check with your instructor to see if this style is acceptable.)
- *Page, document, volume, and issue numbers.* When citing a portion of a larger work or site, list the inclusive page numbers or document numbers of the specific item being cited. For journals or journal articles, include volume and issue numbers.
- *Length.* The length may be shown as a total page count, such as *85 p.* For much electronic material, length is approximate and is shown in square brackets, such as *[12 paragraphs]* or *[about 6 screens].*
- *Address.* Include the URL or other electronic address; use the phrase *Available from:* to introduce the address.

13. ELECTRONIC BOOKS (MONOGRAPHS)

[13]Johnson KA, Becker JA. The whole brain atlas [Internet]. Boston: Harvard Medical School; c1995-1999 [modified 1999 Jan 12; cited 2001 Mar 7]. Available from: http://www.med.harvard.edu/AANLIB/home.html

To cite a portion of an online book, include the name of the part after the date cited. Include page numbers, if available. If no page numbers are available, include an estimated length for the part, and end with a period: *Chapter 6, Degenerative disease [about 2 screens].*

14. ELECTRONIC JOURNAL ARTICLES

Include the authors' names; the title of the article; the title of the journal; the word *Internet* in brackets; as full a date of publication as possible; the date of access; the volume, issue, and page numbers (using designations such as *[16 paragraphs]* or *[5 screens]* if traditional page numbering is not available); and the URL.

[14]Tong V, Abbot FS, Mbofana S, Walker MJ. In vitro investigation of the hepatic extraction of RSD1070, a novel antiarrhythmic compound. J Pharm Pharmaceut Sci [Internet]. 2001 [cited 2001 Oct 15]; 4(1):15-23. Available from: http://www.ualberta.ca/~csps/JPPS4(1)/F.Abbott/RSD1070.pdf

15. WORLD WIDE WEB SITE

Include as many of the following dates as possible: the date of publication (or, if this is not available, the copyright date preceded by *c*); the date of the most recent revision; and the date of access.

[15]Animal Welfare Information Center [Internet]. Beltsville, MD: National Agricultural Library (US); [updated 2001 Oct 11; cited 2001 Oct 15]. Available from: http://www.nal.usda.gov/awic

[16]Hypertension, Dialysis & Clinical Nephrology [Internet]. Hinsdale, IL: Medtext; c1995-2001 [cited 2001 Oct 15]. Available from: http://www.medtext.com/hdcn.htm

16. MATERIAL FROM AN ONLINE DATABASE

If the database is open—with records still being added to it—include the beginning date for the database (*2000–*), or include a dash after the date of publication.

```
17Envirofacts Warehouse. Washington, DC:
    Environmental Protection Agency; [updated
    2001 Aug 13; cited 2001 Oct 15]. Toxic
    releases [about 2 paragraphs]. Available
    from: http://www.epa.gov/enviro
    /html/toxic_releases.html
18Ovid [Internet]. New York: Ovid Technologies.
    c2000-2001 - [cited 2001 May 3]. Available
    from: http://gateway.ovid.com/. Subscription
    required.
```

17. EMAIL

Include the author's name; the subject line of the message; the word *Internet* in square brackets; the words *Message to:* followed by the addressee's name; information about when the email was sent and when it was cited; and the length of the message.

```
19Voss J. Questions about CBE style [Internet].
    Message to: Stephanie Carpenter. 2002 Jan
    29, 3:34 pm [cited 2002 Jan 30]. [about 1
    screen]
```

18. POSTING TO A DISCUSSION GROUP

Begin with the author's name, the subject line, and the name of the discussion list or group, and include as much of the following information as possible.

[20]Rooyer L. Routing BRM. In: DOCLINE-L
    [Internet]. Bethesda, MD: National Library
    of Medicine (US); 2001 Apr 2, 21:17:35
    [cited 2001 Oct 15]. [about 2 paragraphs].
    Available from: DOCLINE-L@LIST.NIH.GOV
    Archives available from: http://
    list.nih.gov/archives/docline-1.html

A Student Research Proposal, CBE Style

The following piece of student writing uses the CBE style (citation-sequence format). The paper is a proposal for a summer research fellowship by Tara Gupta, a student at Colgate University.

Field Measurements of
Photosynthesis and Transpiration
Rates in Dwarf Snapdragon
(*Chaenorrhinum minus* Lange):
An Investigation of Water Stress
Adaptations

Tara Gupta

Proposal for a
Summer Research Fellowship
Colgate University
February 25, 2003

Water Stress Adaptations 2

Introduction

Dwarf snapdragon (*Chaenorrhinum minus*) is a weedy pioneer plant found growing in central New York during spring and summer. Interestingly, the distribution of this species has been limited almost exclusively to the cinder ballast of railroad tracks[1] and to sterile strips of land along highways.[2] In these harsh environments, characterized by intense sunlight and poor soil water retention, one would expect *C. minus* to exhibit anatomical features similar to those of xeromorphic plants (species adapted to arid habitats).

However, this is not the case. T. Gupta and R. Arnold (unpublished) have found that the leaves and stems of *C. minus* are not covered by a thick, waxy cuticle but rather with a thin cuticle that is less effective in inhibiting water loss through diffusion. The root system is not long and thick, capable of reaching deeper, moister soils; instead, it is thin and diffuse, permeating only the topmost (and driest) soil horizon. Moreover, in contrast to many xeromorphic plants, the stomata (pores regulating gas exchange) are not found in sunken crypts or cavities in the epidermis that retard water loss from transpiration.

Water Stress Adaptations 3

Despite a lack of these morphological adaptations to water stress, *C. minus* continues to grow and reproduce when morning dew has been its only source of water for up to five weeks (R. Arnold, personal communication). Such growth involves fixation of carbon by photosynthesis and requires that the stomata be open to admit sufficient carbon dioxide. Given the dry, sunny environment, the time required for adequate carbon fixation must also mean a significant loss of water through transpiration as open stomata exchange carbon dioxide with water. How does *C. minus* balance the need for carbon with the need to conserve water?

Purposes of the Proposed Study

The above observations have led me to an exploration of the extent to which *C. minus* is able to photosynthesize under conditions of low water availability. It is my hypothesis that *C. minus* adapts to these conditions by photosynthesizing in the early morning and late afternoon, when leaf and air temperatures are lower and transpirational water loss is reduced. During the middle of the day, its photosynthetic rate may be very low, perhaps even zero, on hot, sunny afternoons. Similar diurnal changes in photosynthetic rate in response to midday water deficits have been described in crop plants.[3,4] There appear to be no comparable studies on noncrop species in their natural habitats.

Thus, the research proposed here aims to help explain the apparent paradox of an organism that thrives in water-stressed conditions despite a lack of morphological adaptations. This summer's work will also serve as a basis for controlled experiments in a plant growth chamber on the individual effects of temperature, light intensity, soil water availability, and other environmental factors on photosynthesis and transpiration rates. These experiments are planned for the coming fall semester.

Methods and Timeline

Simultaneous measurements of photosynthesis and transpiration rates will indicate the balance *C. minus* has achieved in acquiring the energy it needs while retaining the water available to it. These measurements will be taken daily from June 22 to September 7, 2003, at field sites in the Hamilton, NY, area, using an LI-6220 portable photosynthesis system (LICOR, Inc., Lincoln, NE). Basic methodology and use of correction factors will be similar to that described in related

Water Stress Adaptations 5

studies.[5-7] Data will be collected at regular intervals throughout the daylight hours and will be related to measurements of ambient air temperature, leaf temperature, relative humidity, light intensity, wind velocity, and cloud cover.

Budget

1 kg soda lime, 4-8 mesh (for absorption of CO_2 in photosynthesis analyzer)	$70
1 kg anhydrous magnesium perchlorate (used as desiccant for photosynthesis analyzer)	$130
SigmaScan software (Jandel Scientific Software, Inc.) (for measurement of leaf areas for which photosynthesis and transpiration rates are to be determined)	$195
Estimated 500 miles travel to field sites in own car @ $0.28/mile	$140
CO_2 cylinder, 80 days rental @ $0.25/day (for calibration of photosynthesis analyzer)	$20
TOTAL REQUEST	$555

Water Stress Adaptations 6

References

[1] Wildrlechner MP. Historical and phenological observations of the spread of *Chaenorrhinum minus* across North America. Can J Bot 1983; 61:179-87.

[2] Dwarf Snapdragon [Internet]. Olympia, WA: Washington State Noxious Weed Control Board; [updated 2001 July 7; cited 2003 Jan 25]. Available from: http://www.wa.gov/agr/weedboard/weed_info/dwarfsnapdragon.html

[3] Boyer JS. Plant productivity and environment. Science 1982;218:443-8.

[4] Manhas JG, Sukumaran NP. Diurnal changes in net photosynthetic rate in potato in two environments. Potato Res 1988;31:375-8.

[5] Doley DG, Unwin GL, Yates DJ. Spatial and temporal distribution of photosynthesis and transpiration by single leaves in a rainforest tree, *Argyrodendron peralatum*. Aust J Plant Physiol 1988;15:317-26.

[6] Kallarackal J, Milburn JA, Baker DA. Water relations of the banana. III. Effects of controlled water stress on water potential, transpiration, photosynthesis and leaf growth. Aust J Plant Physiol 1990;17:79-90.

Water Stress Adaptations 7

[7] Idso SB, Allen SG, Kimball BA, Choudhury BJ. Problems with porometry: measuring net photosynthesis by leaf chamber techniques. Agron 1989;81:475-9.

8
Research in the Applied Sciences

Resources in the Applied Sciences

GENERAL REFERENCE SOURCES FOR THE APPLIED SCIENCES

Encyclopedia of Physical Science and Technology. 18 vols. 2002. Consists of over 700 entries, each approximately 20 pages in length, on topics such as molecular electronics, image-guided surgery, fiber-optic chemical sensors, self-organizing systems, humanoid robots, pharmacokinetics, and superstring theory.

The International Encyclopedia of Science and Technology. 2000. Includes over 6,500 entries with graphs, photos, and diagrams; a detailed timeline of the development of science since 2500 B.C.; and a reference section of tables such as SI units, chemical elements, facts about the earth, lists of constellations, and Nobel prize winners.

INDEXES AND DATABASES FOR THE APPLIED SCIENCES

Applied Science and Technology Index. 1958–. Formerly *Industrial Arts Index*, 1913–57. Indexes and abstracts (on CD-ROM) nearly four hundred periodicals, concentrating on applied science in areas such as computers, construction, electronics, engineering, the environment, energy sources, geology, technology, telecommunications, and many others. (online by subscription, CD-ROM)

Government Reports: Announcements and Index. 1971–. Indexes and abstracts reports handled through the National Technical Information Service. (online by subscription)

Scientific and Technical Information Sources. 1987. Lists resources available in the pure and applied sciences.

WEB RESOURCES FOR THE APPLIED SCIENCES

EurekAlert! Your Global Gateway to Science, Medicine, and Technology News
<http://www.eurekalert.org>
Posts, under the sponsorship of the American Association for the Advancement of Science, news of scientific and technological research advances; also includes glossaries, dictionaries, and other reference materials for agriculture, computer sciences, environmental studies, and other fields.

Infomine: Scholarly Internet Resource Collections
<http://lib-www.ucr.edu>
Supplies indexed and annotated links to more than one thousand databases and other resources of academic interest in the physical sciences, including engineering, environmental studies, and computer sciences.

New Scientist
<http://www.newscientist.com/weblinks/>
Supplies engaging annotated links to selected sites, often on specialized topics, in fields including technology, the Internet, and the environment.

LSU Subject Guides
<http://www.lib.lsu.edu/weblio.html>
Provides extensive annotated guides to Web resources in the applied sciences, including agriculture, computer science, environmental studies, food science, human ecology, and other specialized fields.

(See also the resources listed for the natural sciences in Chapter 7.)

Agriculture

GENERAL REFERENCE SOURCES FOR AGRICULTURE

Agriculture Handbooks. 1950–. Each volume supplies reliable information on a specific topic.

Encyclopedia of Agricultural Science. 4 vols. 1994. Contains 210 alphabetically arranged articles, each about 10 pages in length, covering subjects such as animal science, soil science, agricultural education, biotechnology, pest management, and water resources; includes tables and illustrations.

Yearbook of Agriculture. 1895–. Supplies chapters on various aspects of the year's topic.

INDEXES AND DATABASES FOR AGRICULTURE

Agriculture: Illustrated Search Strategy and Sources. 1992. Supplies guidance about using print and electronic reference materials related to agriculture.

Bibliography of Agriculture. 1942–. Indexes thousands of sources from periodicals, state and federal publications, and reports covering agriculture and related topics. (online by subscription, CD-ROM in *AGRICOLA*)

CRIS/ICAR. 1975–. Supplies information about U.S. and Canadian government-sponsored research on agricultural topics. (CD-ROM)

WEB RESOURCES FOR AGRICULTURE

Agricultural Research Service: United States Department of Agriculture
<http://www.ars.usda.gov>
Supplies news and research information as well as links to major agriculture databases and resources, including the National Agricultural Library.

CRIS: Current Research Information Service
<http://cris.csrees.usda.gov>
Reports, under the auspices of the U.S. Department of Agriculture, on thousands of current federal and state research projects on agriculture, forestry, food, and nutrition.

CSU Bioweb: California State University Biological Sciences Web Server
<http://arnica.csustan.edu>
Links to many resources on specialized biological fields such as agriculture, including government resources, multimedia information, and other useful servers and sites.

National Agricultural Library
<http://www.nal.usda.gov/>
Provides its own collection of materials and images on agriculture, and consolidates access to resources through AgNIC (Agriculture Network Information Center) and other Web sites on animal science, economics, food science, forestry, natural resources, nutrition, range land, and other agriculture-related topics.

(See also the resources listed for the life sciences in Chapter 7 on the natural sciences.)

Computer Science

GENERAL REFERENCE SOURCES FOR COMPUTER SCIENCE

Computer Science Sourcebook. 1987. Supplies concise discussions of major topics related to computer programs and software, networks, systems, and computation.

Dictionary of Computer Science, Engineering, and Technology. 2001. Provides detailed definitions for over 8,000 terms that cover topics such as telecommunication, information theory, artificial intelligence, programming language, privacy issues, and software and hardware systems.

Dictionary of Computing. 2001. Defines over 10,000 terms, concepts, and technologies from various areas of computing, such as software, hardware, networking, mainframes, the Internet, multimedia, and programming. (CD-ROM)

McGraw-Hill Encyclopedia of Electronics and Computers. 1988. Includes heavily illustrated articles on the design, materials, functioning, and uses of electronic devices.

Prentice-Hall Encyclopedia of Information Technology. 1987. Supplies articles on a wide range of topics, including languages, components (such as monitors), and applications (such as bar codes and telephone networks).

INDEXES AND DATABASES FOR COMPUTER SCIENCE

ACM Guide to Computing Literature. 1980–. Formerly *ACM Bibliography and Subject Index*, 1963–76. Indexes articles about data, computation, hardware, software, systems, applications, and other computer-related topics. (online by subscription as *ACMPortal*)

WEB RESOURCES FOR COMPUTER SCIENCE

The Collection of Computer Science Bibliographies
  <http://liinwww.ira.uka.de/bibliography/index.html>
  Provides access to over one thousand bibliographies on computer technology, programming, and research, with references to articles, reports, and presentations arranged by subject area.

Developer.com
  <http://softwaredev.earthweb.com>
  Supplies career information, free graphics, and access to thousands of resources on computer technology and topics such as servers, databases, and Web sites, all oriented to professional computer developers.

PC Webopedia
  <http://www.pcwebopedia.com>
  Provides keyword and topical searches on a vast range of terms and topics related to personal computers and computing technology.

WWW Virtual Library—Computing
  <http://www.vlib.org/Computing.html>
  Includes access to bibliographies, indexes, and a dictionary of computer terminology, as well as resources in specialty areas as diverse as artificial intelligence, telecommunications, computational linguistics, and cryptography.

Engineering

GENERAL REFERENCE SOURCES FOR ENGINEERING

Annual Book of ASTM Standards. 1990–. Supplies many volumes, published annually, that detail the specifications, practices, and other guidelines necessary to meet the standards of the American Society for Testing and Materials (ASTM) for products as diverse as plastics, paint, soap, metals and alloys, textiles, and paper.

ASTM Dictionary of Engineering, Science & Technology. 2000. Supplies concise definitions derived from technical committee–developed standards for ASTM terminology.

CRC Handbook of Tables for Applied Engineering Science. 1973. Provides basic tables and data for the various engineering fields.

Encyclopedia of Materials Science and Engineering. 8 vols. 1986. Supplies entries on the nature and use of fibers, plastics, and other materials.

Handbook of Engineering Fundamentals. 1990. Provides essential information for the varied fields of engineering, including equations, laws, theorems, properties, and statistical data.

Handbook of Industrial Engineering. 2001. Includes formulas and data for industrial engineering.

The Illustrated Dictionary of Electronics. 2001. Provides over 27,500 definitions, many with illustrations, of terms in fields that include computers, robotics, lasers, TV, radio, and IC technology.

IEEE 100: The Authoritative Dictionary of IEEE Standards Terms. 2000. Supplies authoritative explanations of terms and standards approved by the Institute of Electrical and Electronics Engineers (IEEE).

Marks' Standard Handbook for Mechanical Engineers. 1987–. Provides essential information for mechanical engineering, including mathematical data, technical standards, and environmental issues.

McGraw-Hill Encyclopedia of Engineering. 1993. Supplies articles on major topics in the many fields of engineering.

Perry's Chemical Engineer's Handbook. 1997. Includes essential specific information for the chemical engineer.

Standard Handbook for Civil Engineers. 1996. Supplies fundamental information for civil engineers, including specifications, construction, design, and management.

Standard Handbook for Electrical Engineers. 1986. Includes necessary reference material for the electrical engineer on topics related to the production, use, and conversion of electrical power.

Standard Handbook of Environmental Engineering. 1990. Supplies essential information about air and water quality, water management, waste disposal, and related topics.

Resources in the Applied Sciences 265

INDEXES AND DATABASES FOR ENGINEERING

Engineering Index Monthly. 1884–. Formerly *Engineering Index*. Indexes and abstracts periodical articles, books, patents, and some conference papers on engineering. (online by subscription, CD-ROM)

INSPEC. 1969–. A database containing citations to journals, conference proceedings, books, reports, and dissertations in physics, electrical engineering and electronics, computers, and information technology. (online by subscription)

WEB RESOURCES FOR ENGINEERING

ASCE's Civil Engineering Database
<http://www.pubs.asce.org/cedbsrch.html>
Provides access to over eighty thousand bibliographic and abstracted records in civil engineering since 1975.

EEVL: The Internet Guide to Engineering, Mathematics and Computing
<http://www.eevl.ac.uk/index.htm>
Provides access to quality networked engineering, mathematics, and computing resources for students, staff, and researchers in higher education.

Electronic Engineers' Toolbox
<http://www.eg3.com/ebox.htm>
A search utility for specialized issues within electronics engineering. Provides links to both commercial and noncommercial resources.

IEEE Spectrum
<http://www.spectrum.ieee.org/>
Provides access to all major publications and resources of the Institute of Electrical and Electronics Engineers.

Institute of Electrical and Electronics Engineers
<http://www.ieee.org>
Links to member services, related technical societies, search engines, databases, publications, and activities.

WWW Virtual Library—Chemical Engineering
<http://www.che.ufl.edu/www-che/>
Offers links to meetings, conferences, organizations, and information resources. Good specific subtopic list.

WWW Virtual Library—Civil Engineering
<http://www.ce.gatech.edu/WWW-CE/home.html>
Lists servers containing information on civil engineering, most of them from university programs.

WWW Virtual Library—Electronics and Electrical Engineering
<http://webdill.cem.itesm.mx/wwwvlee>
A good place to start.

WWW Virtual Library—Engineering
<http://www.eevl.ac.uk/wwwvl.html>
Lists links to many relevant sources across engineering fields, including all the engineering virtual libraries, from acoustic engineering to welding engineering. Includes information on standards, products, and institutions.

Mechanical Design Engineering Resources
<http://www.gearhob.com>
Lists everything from industry associations to research and development sites.

Environmental Studies

GENERAL REFERENCE SOURCES FOR ENVIRONMENTAL STUDIES

A Dictionary of Ecology, Evolution, and Systematics. 1998. Defines over 11,000 concepts, methodologies, and strategies in disciplines such as botany, zoology, bacteriology, mineralogy, and paleontology.

Dictionary of Energy. 1988. Supplies entries with illustrations defining energy-related terms and drawing on scientific, technological, engineering, and economics viewpoints.

Encyclopedia of Environmental Science. 2000. Includes over 340 entries on subjects ranging from alkalinity, dams and reservoirs, and ecological modeling in forestry to renewable resources, urban ecology, and volcanoes.

Encyclopedia of Environmental Science and Technology. 2 vols. 2000. Supplies extensive articles on many aspects of this field, ranging from environmental law and urban planning to hydrology, microbiology, and sulfur removal.

Facts on File Dictionary of Environmental Science. 1991. Includes brief entries on key terms in environmental studies and related fields, such as engineering, law, and computer modeling.

Grzimek's Encyclopedia of Ecology. 1976–. Supplies chapters and maps on such topics as habitats, environmental factors, pollutants, and other influences on the environments of both animals and humans.

McGraw-Hill Encyclopedia of Environmental Science and Engineering. 1993. Provides introductory essays and extensive alphabetical entries on major topics in environmental studies; includes references and illustrations.

United States Energy Atlas. 1986. Supplies explanatory text, figures, and other illustrations with maps to analyze and locate available energy resources.

Water Encyclopedia. 1990. Covers water-related topics such as use, quality, management, and legislation; includes maps, illustrations, and statistical data.

INDEXES AND DATABASES FOR ENVIRONMENTAL STUDIES

Ecological Abstracts. 1980–. Indexes and abstracts articles from over two thousand periodicals and books. (online by subscription, CD-ROM)

Environment Abstracts. 1971–. Supplies abstracts of articles from over five thousand periodicals on topics such as natural resources, pollution, energy, ecology, wildlife, and related areas. (CD-ROM as *ENVIRO/ENERGYLINE*)

Environmental Periodicals Bibliography. 1972–. Lists the contents of hundreds of periodicals, including popular publications, on environmental topics such as natural resources, ecology, air quality, and energy. (online by subscription, CD-ROM)

Pollution Abstracts. 1970–. Supplies abstracts of articles from journals and nontechnical publications about air, water, and other types of pollution, as well as waste management, sewage treatment, radiation, noise control, and related topics. (online by subscription, CD-ROM)

WEB RESOURCES FOR ENVIRONMENTAL STUDIES

CIESIN: Information for a Changing World
   <http://www.ciesin.org>
   Provides scientific data, interactive services, guides to major environmental topics, and access to other resources on the global environment and environmental resources, all under the auspices of the Consortium for International Earth Science Information Network.

EnviroInfo: Environmental Information Sources
   <http://www.deb.uminho.pt/fontes/enviroinfo>
   Provides links to many resources useful for environmental studies of air, water, soil, pollution, waste, ecology, legal issues, and other topics.

EnviroLink
   <http://www.envirolink.org>
   Supplies interactive services, news, and educational and activist information, as well as many links to environmental resources, broadly defined and grouped by category.

EPA: U.S. Environmental Protection Agency
   <http://www.epa.gov>
   Organizes environmental information for various types of users (including citizens, students, and researchers) and by topic (such as news, projects, and publications), including other resources, clearinghouses, and databases.

National Geophysical Data Center
   <http://www.ngdc.noaa.gov>
   Consolidates information—including satellite data—for environmental and related studies.

The WWW Virtual Library: Environment
   <http://www.earthsystems.org/virtuallibrary/vlhome.html>
   Organizes access to resources alphabetically and topically for the study of a broad range of environmental issues.

AIP Style

The *AIP Style Manual* is used by writers in the sciences and applied sciences, including those in the fields of physics, applied physics, optics, astrophysics, and acoustics:

American Institute of Physics. *AIP Style Manual*. 4th ed. New York: American Institute of Physics, 1990.

Many journals and fields in the applied sciences use modifications of the AIP style or their own preferred methods for documenting sources and formatting papers. The various branches of engineering, for instance, have different requirements for citations. If your instructor does not specify a style, be sure to ask which one is preferred in that field.

DIRECTORY TO AIP STYLE

In-Text Notes

List of Notes

BOOKS

1. Book by one author, *270*
2. Book by two or three authors, *271*
3. Book by more than three authors, *271*
4. Book by a corporate or group author, *271*
5. Several sections cited from one edited book in one note, *271*

PERIODICALS

6. Article in a journal paginated by volume, *272*
7. Article in a journal paginated by issue, *272*
8. Article citation including title, *272*
9. Several articles by the same author(s) in the same journal, *272*
10. Several articles by the same author(s) in different journals, *273*
11. Several articles by different author(s) in the same journal, *273*

(Continued)

> **ELECTRONIC SOURCES**
>
> 12. Computer program, 273   13. Internet source, 273
>
> **OTHER SOURCES**
>
> 14. Personal communication, 274

AIP Format for In-Text Notes

The AIP recommends using in-text notes—superscript numbers in the text, numbered consecutively—to mark citations of sources. The references to which the superscript numbers refer are then presented in a double-spaced list of notes at the end of the paper, following the same numerical order. A single number and note may refer to several sources as long as all of them are relevant to the point in the text.

```
      The preliminary work by Grever[1] and Martino[2]
 defined the essential experimental variables.
 Later studies by Throckworth et al.[3] and Wixell[4]
 have confirmed the validity of this approach.
```

AIP Format for a List of Notes

Books

1. BOOK BY ONE AUTHOR

Supply the author's name, initials only or spelled out in full, just as it is on the title page.

[1] J. A. Poppiti, Practical Techniques for Laboratory Analysis (Lewis, Boca Raton, FL, 1994), p. 35.

2. BOOK BY TWO OR THREE AUTHORS

[2] M. Born and E. Wolf, Principles of Optics, 6th ed. (Pergamon, Oxford, 1980), p. 143.

3. BOOK BY MORE THAN THREE AUTHORS

Use *et al.* freely in the text of your paper, but avoid it in the list of notes unless there are three or more authors.

[3] Lillian Hoddeson et al., Critical Assembly: A Technical History of Los Alamos During the Oppenheimer Years, 1943-45 (Cambridge University Press, New York, 1993).

4. BOOK BY A CORPORATE OR GROUP AUTHOR

[4] American National Standards Institute, American National Standard for Human Factors Engineering of Visual Display Terminal Workstations, ANSI/HFS 100-1988 (Human Factors Society, Santa Monica, CA, 1988).

5. SEVERAL SECTIONS CITED FROM ONE EDITED BOOK IN ONE NOTE

[5] John J. Sarraille and Thomas A. Gentry, in Computer-Mediated Communication and the Online

Classroom, edited by Zane L. Berge and Mauri P. Collins (Hampton Press, Cresskill, NJ, 1995), Chap. 9, pp. 137-150; Raleigh C. Muns, ibid., Chap. 10, pp. 151-164.

Periodicals

6. ARTICLE IN A JOURNAL PAGINATED BY VOLUME

[6] S. J. Lee, K. Imen, and S. D. Allen, J. Appl. Phys. **74**, 7046 (1993).

7. ARTICLE IN A JOURNAL PAGINATED BY ISSUE

Check with your instructor about whether you should include page numbers for an entire article or a specific page reference.

[7] John Reason, Elec. World **207** (7), 33-42 (1993).

8. ARTICLE CITATION INCLUDING TITLE

Check with your instructor about whether you should or should not include article titles.

[8] S. J. Lee, K. Imen, and S. D. Allen, "Shock wave analysis or laser assisted particle removal," J. Appl. Phys. **74**, 7046 (1993).

9. SEVERAL ARTICLES BY THE SAME AUTHOR(S) IN THE SAME JOURNAL

[9] Zhiqiang Wu and P. Paul Ruber, J. Appl. Phys. **74**, 6240 (1993); **71**, 1318 (1992).

10. SEVERAL ARTICLES BY THE SAME AUTHOR(S) IN DIFFERENT JOURNALS

[10] S. M. Gates, J. Phys. Chem. **96**, 10439-10443 (1992); Surface Sci. **195**, 307 (1988).

11. SEVERAL ARTICLES BY DIFFERENT AUTHOR(S) IN THE SAME JOURNAL

Use <u>ibid.</u> to show that the articles are "in the same place."

[11] A. C. Kibblewhite and C. Y. Wu, J. Acoust. Soc. Am. **94**, 3376 (1993); G. Haralabus et al., ibid. **94**, 3385 (1993).

Electronic Sources

12. COMPUTER PROGRAM

If the author's name is known, add it to the citation.

[12] SuperCalc3 Release 2.1 (Computer Associates, Micro Products Division, San Jose, CA, 1985).

13. INTERNET SOURCE

The *AIP Style Manual* does not provide guidelines for citing source material from the Internet, and different journals published by the AIP follow different guidelines for such sources. Here are examples of citations that have appeared in such journals.

[13] M. Steyvers and J.B. Tenenbaum, 2001, preprint, www-psych.stanford.edu/~jbt/.

[13] P. Baran, Introduction to Distributed Communications Networks, RM-3420-PR, August 1964,

http://www.rand.org/publications/RM/baran.list.html.

Other Sources

14. PERSONAL COMMUNICATION

[14] J. Kincaid (private communication).